LAST, LEAST, LOWEST:
God's Challenge for Women

LAST, LEAST, LOWEST:
God's Challenge for Women

by Julia Marie Taylor

New Leaf Press, Inc.
Harrison, Arkansas

First Edition

Library of Congress Catalog Card Number: 78-70663
International Standard Book Number: 0-89221-058-3

DEDICATION

I dedicate this book to all of the women who are part of the loud cry and are searching to become complete and free according to the Word of God.

And he sat down, and called the twelve, and saith unto them, If any man desire to be first, the same shall be last of all, and servant of all.

—Mark 9:35

ACKNOWLEDGMENTS

I want to give special thanks to:
- All the young women and young men who have lived at the House of Prayer and Praise. It is through their lives that I have grown and learned how to teach them in the Holy Spirit.
- My own daughters—Judy Hatch, Betty Hayner and Robin Hooker.
- My sons—James Kenny and Dwight Kenny.
- The young women at HOPP—Robin Paulin, Barb Boyer, Nancy Rhodes, Beth Connlly, Ethel Branch, Tina Harris, Linda Wheeler, Marla Sanders, Lagatha Smallwood and Michelle William.
- The young men—David Staab, Dave Ife, Jerry Hooker, Dan Douglas, Chester Pipkin, Zave Levi and Brenda McHenry.
- All the young people at Rejoice Ministries in L.A. at Pepperdine University, UCLA and Whittier College, and thousands of others too.
- A special acknowledgment to Jim Wallace, Bud Parriott, Jim Sheppard, and especially to Cliff Dudley and Becky Phillips.
- Most of all thank you to my own precious mother, Mary Rucker Carlton, an untarnished saint, at LaVergne, Tennessee. I love her, and thank her for praying for me.

CONTENTS

Page

PREFACE

This book is the answer to the dreadful cry of young women around the world. The teaching is based on the Biblical book of Titus, centering specifically on Chapter Two. I believe women should be women according to the Word of God and not according to our fast-moving and out-of-control society. It is the purpose of this book to show women how they can be true women of God and by so doing, become the best helpmate a husband can have, also the best mother that a child can have.

This book offers women, both young and old alike, a much richer and fuller life with their husbands, children, and with themselves. After finishing my first book, *God's Kids and Mom,* the Lord took me into the inner court of Heaven and there Jesus instructed me to seek out the older women who are guiding the young girls according to the Bible principles. I looked hard but could not find any such women and thus called again unto the Lord concerning the matter. He said, "You teach them."

"I'm not an older woman, " I replied.

The Lord then said, "Call the mourning women," but the result was the same. The Lord did not stop there. He instructed me to take hold of the leadership and call the young daughters and teach them according to the Word of God, to pray like the weeping and mourning women of

Jeremiah's time.

At first I could not find older women, or young women who would pray as prayer warriors. For some time my own young daughter and young sons had to agree in prayer with me. The burden for young women got heavier and their cry for help got louder.

In Proverbs 21:13 the Word says, "Whoso stoppeth his ears at the cry of the poor, he also shall cry himself, but shall not be heard." This cry is a cry of the poor. Who are the poor? It is those in need. The young women are in need; in fact, it is the heaviest need I know of right now. They haven't been taught anything that helps them to be women of God like the Bible teaches.

Therefore, this book was written with the concern and belief that God has called upon women to return to Jesus Christ, make Him their first love, forget all these games with men, God and themselves. Quit trying to be something that they are not, and never were supposed to be, and cannot be in God's Kingdom.

Is Jesus the Lord of your life? If not, why not?

—Julia Marie Taylor

Chapter 1

I HEAR A CRY

I hear a cry.

I hear a cry everywhere I go.

I hear this cry, the cry of the young women.

It's from Germany, Israel, China, Italy, and everywhere I go.

The cry of:

Who am I?

Where do I belong?

Where can I find security?

Why am I on earth?

Maybe I should have never been born.

I need something. I need someone to help me.

The cry I am hearing is coming from the young women of all ages. It's even into the small young women of grammar school, and it's demanding an answer, and the answer must come soon.

I hear the black women saying, "My time has run out. Nobody cares for me. I heard my forefathers talking hate, hate, hate. I heard my grandma's talking hate. Now the sin of the fourth generation is come upon me. Where can I turn to, who will care for me? I've been into prostitution."

I hear the cry of the young woman saying, "There's

books for everybody else, but what about me? I've been into all kinds of heavy sins. I've been with the pimps, and I was the pimps' first lady. Maybe I was a first-class prostitute, but it's still low class in Jesus. Who will help me?"

I hear the cry of the women coming out of the mental institutions: "There's no place for me to go. The churches won't have me. My parents won't have me. Drugs have messed me up, and no man will have me because I am now a schizophrenic. Oh, God, send somebody to help me."

I hear this cry. I hear it in the morning, all day, and every night. A cry of the young girl in a Christian school that is on drugs, but doesn't want her parents to know it. She can't tell the pastor and she can't tell her parents, but she really wants to be set free: "Help me, help me. I know I'm not living the life that I should, there is something wrong. I see too many phonies in the church. Help me."

The cry goes on and on.

A young girl who sees her parents fighting, slips out at night to have sex with her boy friend, and yet comes home miserable and bound up. I hear the cry: "My God, my God, is there no one to help me?"

Women today are not like they used to be in our mothers' and our grandmothers' day. They had God-fearing husbands who ruled their households with the authority of the Word. Men were boss and wore the pants in the family. Women had large families and they had happy homes. They were happy raising children, and being a handmaiden. These were her aims and her joys. Now it seems becoming equal with men, or beating them in a race, or getting above them is her goal. The woman's role seems so artificial, so unreal, that it leaves her in a state of loneliness and despair. Instead of domestic concern being the central theme in a woman's life, it now seems to be the equalization to that of manhood—it is called Women's Free Liberation.

If you have read my last book entitled *God's Kids and Mom* you will be aware of the open house policy I operate in my home in Garden Grove, California. Most of the young girls who come into my home to live have never been taught. They have never been taught to cook or clean house. They don't know how to handle a needle or sew. They've never taken responsibility of any kind. I had one young girl whose mother was an alcoholic, and as a young girl she had made up her mind never to take responsibility because she could still remember the sirens as the ambulance came to pick up her mother in a drunken stupor to take her to the hospital. She was the only one to go along in the ambulance with her.

Most young girls have never been made to mind, respect authority, or to have been corrected in any way. Yet they all have mothers and fathers somewhere.

Millie, who lived with us for nine months said one night when she came home loaded with Reds and Pot, her mother just patted her on the back and said, "Honey, it will be all right."

It wasn't all right, because the girl really wanted her mother to correct and to chastise her, and to tell her the right way. It is God's law and His Word that says God loves those whom He chastens, and that's what the girl really wanted.

The young women today have learned much about beauty aids, secrets of primping, and new ways of putting on make-up, spending hours on end experimenting with powders, lipsticks, and all kinds of blush, cover-ups, etc. Yet most of them have never learned the secret beauty of the heart which shines from within that makes the eyes and face glow with a joy and contentment that cannot be covered up. We can try everything on the market and search the world over looking for things to change the outward appearance, but it never can do the job, only Jesus can. *Real beauty doesn't come until there is a change in the heart.*

Yes, I hear them crying, "Teach me, teach me, I want the truth. I want happiness." I hear them asking, "Should I have a career? Should I get married, or just live with my boy friend?"

Women are searching for freedom. "I want to be free," they cry. Yet I say there is no freedom out of God's law; there is only bondage. But they answer, "What do you mean God's law? I demand equal rights with men. I've got my rights to be free from men, and equal to them." You may think you have that right; it is a counterfeit right. It does not come from God or Jesus Christ our risen Saviour. It comes from Satan. He is the enemy to God. He is the counterfeit and the father of lies. So guess where Free Liberation came from? You are right! You guessed it, Satan is the father of lies. There is no truth in him nor in Women's Free Liberation. He makes you think you are free just so he can bind you up for eternity. Yes, there is an answer in the truth of God's Word to all the questions of young women of today. There is a *place* for you and a great *need* for you. Jesus loves you so much and has always had a perfect plan for each person.

First of all, we have to get into His Word, the Bible (which is the truth—Jesus says, He "is the way, the truth and the life"), and take it by faith, listen to it, put on the Word and live it. We do not go by what we feel, or what others may do or tell us to do. We already have a blueprint to follow concerning how to live this Christian life—the holy Word of God. It is a road map that leads to Heaven and eternal life, yet it has all the answers to love, peace, joy, patience and longsuffering—that which gives us happiness on this earth.

Sue, a young girl of fifteen years, lived in my home under my guidance, but had never experienced a spanking. She had been left to do as she pleased most of her life. At an early age she started being torn emotionally by her father and mother, which resulted in her being placed in various orphanages time and again. By the time she got to my house she was very mentally disturbed. But the kids and I showed much love to her. One day in particular, she seemed especially spaced out and would not listen to anything being said. My patience was very thin and I scolded her pretty hard. It always hurts to scold one of God's creations, but sometimes it is necessary. Soon after the scolding I went to her room and kissed her on the forehead saying, "Sue, that is because I love you." I wanted Sue to feel she was not being picked on. Expecting an understanding gesture from her, I went on to describe how I spanked my own son that very day with a belt because I loved him.

She looked directly at me, and I heard her cry inside, "Why didn't you whip me? Don't you love me like you do your own son?"

Sue's words went deep into my heart, so I took her to the bedroom and spanked her. She cried for joy because now she knew I loved her.

The cry is loud and it is getting louder, and the questions are getting harder. The urgency for answers is long overdue. Today in our society, a society which is made up of more than 240,000 illegitimate births each year in the United States alone, needs to help its young women who are losing perspective of what is right and wrong. Yes! I have heard the cry! And the following pages are going to attempt to direct the crying women back to the original source of answers which brought so much contentment to the women of yesteryear.

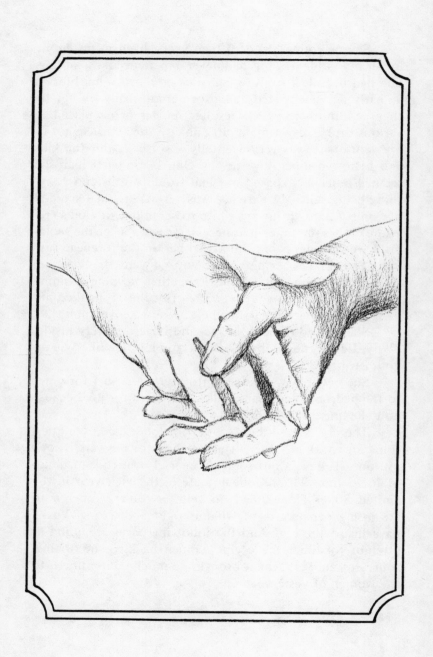

Chapter 2

IT STARTED WITH ADAM

Don't let this title bother you; just because Adam happened to be created first by God does not mean he was any better than Eve. If position of creation implies superiority among the created, then everything in this world is more important than mankind. For man was created last— on the sixth day (Genesis 1:26).*

Adam being created first placed certain responsibilities upon him, such as being instructed personally by God concerning the warning of eating fruit from the tree of the knowledge of good and evil (Genesis 2:17), and the naming of all of the living creatures which God created on the earth (Genesis 2:19). These responsibilities demanded explanations from Adam to Eve, his soon-to-be created wife. This was the first sign of man's leadership role in the marriage relationship; the role of an instructor.

Adam was God's perfect creation, but that perfect creation had one flaw—he suffered from loneliness and didn't even know why. God's great love saw this loneliness in man, and it was at this time, we girls came upon the

---

*Scriptures (KJV) referred to are typed out in full at end of each chapter.

scene. God, the great God and creator of all things, placed Adam in a deep sleep for the purpose of creating a woman (Eve). He created Eve not from the dust of the ground or from some precious metal to be looked upon as some type of rare value, but He created her from an actual rib from Adam's side (Genesis 2:22). He did this for a reason. The more man loves himself the more he must love us girls, for we are truly a part of him. It has been so beautifully stated by the poet:

A woman—not made from his head, to rule over him; not out of his feet to be trampled on by him; but out of his side to be equal with him; under his arm to be protected; and near his heart to be loved.

Adam needed a helpmate, and God created one for him. He was not searching for a helpmate at the time—matter of fact, he did not even realize he needed one—he was busy about his Father's business. God saw Adam's need and took action. Our God is a God of action, and He will never let you down. Men should not be searching for a helpmate but have their eyes fixed upon God. This was the beginning of woman—a helpmate for man. But this position demands responsibility from the woman.

Many young marriages end up in divorce simply because the woman does not know what it means to be a helpmate. First, Eve was added to Adam by God, not just a rib taken from him. This means, a woman should become part of what is already going on. Add to it, be a reason for his advancing, not work against the husband but work with him. The woman must be willing to accept God's creative plan of placing upon man the responsibility of the leadership role. The type of leadership I am referring to does not mean blind guidance but means responsible guidance and allegiance with each other. Even though you do not see the good in your husband now, you should

20

continue to try to bring forth the good until it comes. If you would truly look up to your husband and obey him, he will love you, protect you and would guard against leading you into danger.

True submission is combined with the "agape" love, the self-sacrificing love, the type of love that is willing to give of itself. Such a love will cause your husband to love you to the point of submission and, therefore, the submission itself will become on your behalf "eager willingness." This is God's way and God's plan for you and your husband. A woman who truly loves her husband will want to spoil him. Girls, if you learn to love Jesus you'll love your husband, but you should also love yourself. You don't just "fall" in love. Rather, you decide to love.

Love is the ability to give without considering what you will receive. Love is wanting to serve.

Love seeks to give all to make the other happy, and gives freedom, does not force or nag.

We love because Jesus first loved us and thus taught us to love. Each wife loves and cares for her husband because her husband loves and cares for her. This continuing cycle grows stronger with each additional instance of care and concern, as long as both keep their eyes upon God.

Adam and Eve were commanded to know each other and replenish the earth. God wanted man and woman to know each other sexually. This seems to be one of the main problems that girls have to deal with. I hear many people today putting down sex as if it were something dirty, or the by-product of some contagious disease. If you don't know it, you had better learn it now: GOD INVENTED SEX, and it is not dirty—only out of wedlock is it dirty. Then it is not only dirty, it is sin and death. Sex is only meant to be in holy matrimony. God never limited it to just the procreation of the human race, it is also an act of pleasure for man and woman. If women are not fulfilling the sexual obligation of marriage then they are virtually destroying it, and you have failed your husband and the responsibility which God has given you. That goes for the husband too. It works both ways (I Corinthians 7:4-5).

I have had many girls come to me saying, "I just can't stand having sex with my husband; all he thinks about is sex and nothing else." All I can say is that you are not giving it your all. If you would give all of your sexual love to your husband, he would be satisfied, and sex would become less of a problem in your relationship and you would begin to enjoy it. God wants you to be a complete helpmate to your husband, not just part of a helpmate, for no part is equal to the whole. Sex was given to you and your husband together. Neither of you owns sex, it is a gift from God. So, never hold back sex from your husband for that is against God's perfect will for you. Remember, a marriage bed should remain undefiled. Undefiled means pure and holy, not *anything goes.* Oral sex in marriage is just as perverted and sinful in marriage as it is out of marriage. It will ruin a good marriage. Natural sex is God's way.

One of the first ingredients that must be applied to foster a God-fearing, healthy relationship is the fear of God. When you speak to your husband, give him a chance to answer, or else no communication has taken place. Remember the Lord's words, "Do unto others as you wish them to do unto you," (even your husband!). Girls like to talk and be heard; so do the husbands! Women, take a back seat, be quiet and let your husband lead. Put on a quiet and meek spirit.

Key Tips for Wives to Remember

Read the Word and pray with and for your husband. Encourage him in the Lord. Your husband is a gift from God—treat him as such. Communicate with him as if he were the only man in the world. Look up to him, adore him. Make him believe that after Jesus, he is the center of your life, and he will be.

If you will reread this chapter and take it to heart and apply it in your relationship with your husband you will find true freedom and love. It is God's will and desire for you to be happy with the feeling of fulfillment and completeness as a woman and a wife. But this calls for complete responsible submission. It is up to you. What will it be?

Gen. 1:26   And God said, Let us make man in our image, after our likeness: and let them have dominion over the fish of the sea, and over the fowl of the air, and over the cattle, and over all the earth, and over every creeping thing that creepeth upon the earth.

2:17   But of the tree of the knowledge of good and evil, thou shalt not eat of it: for in the day that thou eatest thereof thou shalt surely die.

2:19   And out of the ground the LORD God formed every beast of the field, and every fowl of the air; and brought them unto Adam to see what he would call them; and whatsoever Adam called every living creature, that was the name thereof.

2:22   And the rib, which the LORD God had taken from man, made he a woman, and brought her unto the man.

I Cor. 7:4-5   The wife hath not power of her own body, but the husband: and likewise also the husband hath not power of his own body, but the wife.

Defraud ye not one the other, except it be with consent for a time, that ye may give yourselves to fasting and prayer; and come together again, that Satan tempt you not for your incontinency.

Chapter 3

OLDER WOMEN

Is there such a creature as an **older** woman? Do you really ever feel old? I do not know, for age is relative with the mental attitude of the person concerned. But, if there is such a thing as older women, then I surely must qualify, even though I feel young in heart.

The concept of older women describes a process of "becoming" in relationship to experience, an experience which caused and fostered a depth of sincerity, patience, longsuffering and, above all, understanding. Therefore, I see the older woman as a person who has experienced all of the facets of life which a young girl must yet live through. The older woman has already lived it, she has breathed and suffered it, she has prayed it, and above all, she has comforted others as she has been comforted herself. If I have not lived it, then how can I teach it? Trusting God, walking and living in the Word is the main requirement.

When I hear the term "older woman," I do not see an old lady bent over, sitting in a rocking chair barely hanging on to the last threads of life, just waiting for her time to end, but a woman with real deep joy in her heart. If we accept the belief that we are too old to be of any use or

25

too young to really have any valuable answers, we choose not to try. We must remember there is no set age in relationship to older women. The only qualifying ingredient is experience, the experience of having children, for surely you are older than the child you bore, and your parents are older than you. As you can see, the term "older women" is relative.

I hope all women think of themselves as being young, but yet maintain the responsibility that experience brings. This responsibility demands sharing of yourself to help younger girls with less experience. I can minister to young girls who are the same age as my own children just as well as I can to the older girls because of my own experience in already having lived it. Therefore, I am at the age of anyone to whom I minister. This is what the Apostle Paul meant when he said, "Be all things to all people." The most important experience though is how long and how much we know and love the Lord.

In the Book of Titus we witness the Apostle Paul warning Titus, a Greek Gentile who was previously converted by Paul, concerning the dangers of the false teaching arising particularly from Judaizers (Titus 1:10-16). Paul, from this background attempts to explain the Christian precepts for various groups in the church which will strengthen the people of God from being misled by false teachers. In so doing he defined the role of "older women" (Titus 2:3-5).

Older women, according to the Apostle Paul, should maintain some of the same attributes and more as the aged men (Titus 2:2). They should be "sober, grave, temperate, sound in faith, in charity, in patience." Their behavior should "become holiness," as priestesses they should not be "false accusers" or "slanderers" (from which the English word "devil" is derived). Paul goes on to say older women should "not be given to much wine." If you have salvation you don't want or need any alcoholic drinks. Stay away from it.

Older women were to be "teachers of good things," in contrast with mere gossip, slander, or "old wives' fables" (I Timothy 4:7).

The reason the Apostle Paul instructed the older women to be such, was to prepare them for the responsibility which God had given them. This responsibility is the physical job of teaching the young women to be "sober," which is literally to teach them common sense and to take spiritual responsibility. They were also instructed to teach the young women how to love their husbands and their children. The sound-minded wife realizes that the harmony and strength of the home depends upon her role as a helper to her husband, not as a competitor. Paul emphasizes the basic law of family security and emotional development. The contribution of a loving, God-fearing mother, consistently and unselfishly offered to every growing child, cannot be fully supplied otherwise.

The young women are to be instructed to be "discreet" and "chaste"; they are taught how to develop self-control and to be prudent at all times. Self-control denotes victory over selfishness. Personal desires are to be made subject to the overall good of the family and others, and disappointments are to be met with the courage of Jesus. The young women are to be taught to be "keepers at home" or "workers at home." Mothers who spend a great portion of time outside of the home sometimes neglect family responsibilities. To allow the children to roam without parental oversight or to place them under the guidance of a paid baby-sitter does not fulfill the divine instruction given in the Word. The young women are also to be taught to be "good" and "obedient" to their husbands in all things, except or unless it be unwise or sinful. By such action, according to the Apostle Paul, the Word of God will not be blasphemed (Titus 2:5).

But, I am asked, "How can an older woman teach a young girl to be such, according to the Word of God?" The only way an older woman can meet and teach a young girl is by getting right up close to her heart. Get to know her; learn to feel her pains and hurts, her loneliness and fear; relate with her in all aspects, and, above all, grow up with her. Make yourself a vital, irreplaceable part of her life; be as a strong, straight stick which is stuck in the ground beside the newly-planted sapling tree for the purpose of holding it up and to be leaned upon. In a short time you will notice the young girl building her life around your example of the Word of God. Just like the little sapling tree which will outgrow and encompass the stick—until the stick itself becomes part of the tree, so will the Word of God become part of her. As you can see, the older woman is not a lady of years but a strong *guidepost of experience* for the young and inexperienced. The older woman is comprised of what she has experienced, done and, above all, shared and lived.

Before the older women should attempt to reach out towards the young girls crying for help, they should make a commitment to God themselves (and later to the young girls) that they will be honest, real and sincere, giving only the truth of the Word and the love of God.

The *ethos* (first impression) of perfectionism, shown by so many adults, does discourage many of the young girls from ever trying to live according to God's Word, for they feel unable to live up to it. They need to see and feel the older woman as being a real person who has experienced hurts, pain, failures, frustration, and anxiety, like themselves. Then they can more likely listen to and heed instruction.

The teaching experience which the older women are instructed to participate in with the young girls is exciting because the young girls are so hungry to learn the answers to their many unanswered questions. They seemingly can't get enough.

The young girls will receive a blessing when they see the older women, whom Jesus loves and adores, permitting them to see all their faults and flaws. The young girls will discover that even though they themselves are not perfect, Jesus will still love them as He loves the older women. Perfectionism in this case will not be a threat and will not discourage the young girls from trying.

A young girl once staying with Pop and me made the remark, "Mom, you and Pop are the only adults that I have seen who had faults—at least the first adults that would admit it."

I answered her saying, "The first two years that Pop and I were married, Pop didn't have any faults." I believe a woman should confess her faults without waiting for her husband to confess his. This is the first sign of humility. Just be real, that's all. Die to your own rights to win the other person.

When I landed in Germany, the new country to which Pass It On Ministries was being introduced, and where my daughter and son-in-law lived, many young people were waiting to meet me. I wondered why they would even take the time to come. I was informed by one of them soon afterward concerning the reason, which was, in her own words, "You are meetable, you are on the same level as we. You don't carry a false front, you are for real, you are sincere, and you know how to communicate with us—you talk to us, you don't just preach to us. You listen to what we have to say!"

The virtues of womanhood are best transmitted from one generation to another by God-fearing, spiritual, and emotionally-mature older women who have learned well the lessons of the Word of God, self-discipline and personal humility. It is tragic for young women to assume the duties of wifehood and motherhood without having been properly taught the responsibilities of Christian womanhood.

Yes, I hear the cry, and it is getting louder and louder, and it is demanding answers from the older women.

Do you hear it?

Do you care?

Will you give your time, love and life to help these dying souls?

Study the Word. Pray. Start at home and go forth.

Titus 1:10	For there are many unruly and vain talkers and deceivers, specially they of the circumcision:
:11	Whose mouths must be stopped; who subvert whole houses, teaching things which they ought not, for filthy lucre's sake.
:12	One of themselves, even a prophet of their own, said, The Cretians are always liars, evil beasts, slow bellies.
:13	This witness is true. Wherefore rebuke them sharply; that they may be sound in the faith;
:14	Not giving heed to Jewish fables, and commandments of men, that turn from the truth.
:15	Unto the pure all things are pure: but unto them that are defiled and unbelieving is nothing pure; but even their mind and conscience is defiled.
:16	They profess that they know God; but in works they deny him, being abominable, and disobedient, and unto every good work reprobate.
2:2	That the aged men be sober, grave, temperate, sound in faith, in charity, in patience.
:3	The aged women likewise, that they be in behaviour as becometh holiness, not false accusers, not given to much wine, teachers of good things.
:4	That they may teach the young women to be sober, to love their husbands, to love their children.
:5	To be discreet, chaste, keepers at home, good, obedient to their own husbands, that the word of God be not blasphemed.

NOTES

Chapter 4

TRAIN UP A CHILD IN THE WAY . . .

Do not think for one minute "correcting" and "disciplining" children is easy. Personally, I believe it is the hardest, but most important, task given to us by God. Yet it is most often neglected because young mothers are scared the child will stop liking them as parents. As if this were the most important thing!

Though many mothers today follow the psychologists' view concerning the raising of their children instead of the Biblical record, they do not believe it is right to even say "no" to their child, for that may destroy the child's will. Therefore, the child grows up becoming obstinate and demanding, and then many parents shirk with fear because they do not understand what has happened to their child. If you don't discipline your child, your child and you will be to the point of ruin.

Mothers, wake up! It is your responsibility to raise your children in the way they should go. Do not think they will develop naturally into the perfect child. It has been my experience, for every near perfect or well-behaved child I have seen, there has been a God-fearing and loving mother behind him or her, giving equal amount of love and discipline. I am not saying, "Fathers do not have a part in the raising of the children." The raising of children is definitely, at its best, a joint cooperation of both the father and the mother. But at this particular time I am addressing the mothers.

Young women must be taught how to correct their children. This is the generation of young people talking back and sassing, showing disregard and practising extreme disobedience to parents.

Being a mother in the highest sense means bringing forth sons of God. This is the objective I have for all the young women reading this book; that you may have the strength and the knowledge to bring forth sons of God.

"Train up a child in the way he should go: and when he is old, he will not depart from it" (Proverbs 22:6). This text is not saying that the child will never depart from the Lord's way, but it is saying when he/she is old, he/she will remember what the mother taught, and then he/she will come back to the Lord's way. If the mother neglected to train the child according to God's way while young then the condition of this text was not fulfilled and the promise may be eternally lost.

If you do not know how to raise and train your baby, ask the Lord and the Holy Spirit; They will teach you right here and now. Do not feel ashamed and embarrassed because you lack understanding in raising your child. Many young mothers today are not raising and training their children correctly because they were never taught the correct way themselves. (If you've failed all the way—praise God, ask forgiveness. He'll give you another chance. He did me!)

But, praise the Lord for young women who had God-fearing parents, who can reflect on their growing up and see God's plan in action. This is what young women should strive for and then your child can look back and see your godly example. This is the responsibility which God has given you—to be as the "older women" recorded in Titus

2:3-5, who were able to teach the young women according to God's ways. Such "older women" are needed today and have always been needed, because young women need on-the-job training at home, about marriage and raising children before they plunge into it.

Submit to God's will concerning the correct procedure in training your child. True submission to God's Word will render true success.

Correcting children starts the very second the baby is born. Mothers who choose to breast-feed babies—be aware of the fact that the baby will have a tendency to bite. It is at this time you need to correct them. A good procedure to use to break this habit is to give them a thump on their hand; they will get the idea as long as you are consistent. **Consistency** plays a very important role in child training. Without it there could be no training. Training a child is like breaking a young Tennessee walking horse. You must meet the challenge the minute it is born and you must stick with it until the job is done.

The Bible tells us that newborn babies are weaker today but wiser. I'm also finding them to be more rebellious when they come out of the womb than ever before. Therefore, children must receive firm discipline at the beginning of their life experience, not after life patterns have been set and conditioned.

When I use the word "discipline," I am referring to 100% "discipline" and 100% "love." The two go hand-in-hand, equally distributed. Firm "discipline" and "love" are the two most important ingredients in raising a child, along with the knowledge of God and His love for us.

Young women, NEVER, but NEVER spank your child when you are angry. When you do spank your child, NEVER use your bare hand but use a rod as God instructed us to do. Your bare hand is part of you, and it will make your child think you do not love him. I am a firm believer in chastising my children; it is of God, but child-beating is of Satan.

Every part of the baby is trainable but the tongue. We must "control" the tongue, we must "influence" the tongue, but we cannot train it. So guard against bad influences upon your child.

When I was a young girl, I must admit my parents brought me up right. My parents were Christians and believed in strong discipline and love. I can remember a few times when I sassed my dad and received the razor strap. After having such a background, you would think I would know how to raise my own children, but I did not always train my children right, especially during the time I was backslidden from God. He gives us mothers second chances and more. I praise the Lord for that!

When my daughter, Judy, was three years old I would let her play outside in the yard with the restriction that she must stay in the yard. One day in particular, after a few minutes had gone by, I noticed it was awful quiet in the yard. So I went out to check on her. She was nowhere to be found. I became frightened, worried and mad all at the same time. I soon found her playing in a sandbox two doors down. When I got her back to the house, I grabbed a switch and spanked her, and told her to sit on the porch until I said she could leave. Knowing Judy and her temperament, I figured she would try to disobey me again, so I watched her through the kitchen window. In a couple of minutes, she slipped off the porch and headed back to the sandbox. I immediately walked over, took her by the hand and brought her back to the porch where she met with the switch again. I instructed her a second time to stay on the porch. This time she mumbled a few things to herself. After a couple of minutes she slipped off again, and the disciplinary action was repeated. Judy did not learn her lesson until after the fourth time she was disciplined.

If you love your children, be consistent in disciplining them, or else it will be of no value to them or you. Remember, the type of discipline you apply, let it be according to the crime; and by the way, it does not pay to see everything they do. Loving is the key, and affection makes them feel needed. Give them a goal to work for, praying and teaching the Word of God. Teach them the stories of Jesus; how He was perfect and was Lord God Himself, but yet He was obedient to both His Heavenly Father and earthly father.

Obedience to parental authority should be started in babyhood and cultivated in youth.

Some parents think that they can let their little ones have their own way in their babyhood, and when they are older they will reason with them; but this is a mistake. Begin on the day the baby's born to teach obedience. Require obedience in your home and school. From their earliest life children should be taught to obey their parents, to respect their word, and to reverence their authority.

Obedience to parents leads to obedience to God. The children who have praying parents have been greatly privileged, for such have an opportunity to know and love God. By the children respecting and rendering obedience to their parents, they may learn how to respect and obey their Heavenly Father. If they walk as children of the light, they will be kind and courteous, loving and respectful to their parents, whom they have seen, and thus be better qualified to love God, whom they have not seen. If they are faithful representatives of their parents, practising the truth through the help given them of God, then by precept and example they will more likely acknowledge the ownership of God and honor Him by a well-ordered life and godly conversation.

Impress upon the minds of your children that the Lord is proving them in this life, to see if they will render obedience to Him with love and reverence. Those who would not be obedient to Christ here would not obey Him in the eternal world.

When I talk about correcting the children, I am talking about their salvation. Lessons on obedience, on respect for authority, need to be repeated often. This kind of work done in the family will be a power for good, and not only will the children be protected from evil and encouraged to love truth and righteousness, but parents will be equally benefited. The work which the Lord requires cannot be done without much serious contemplation on the part of the parents and much study of the Word of God in order that they may instruct according to His directions.

Children do not learn just from teaching, preaching and training, but mostly from example. Emerson said it the best, "character is caught, not taught." Dorothy Law Nolte applied the same concept in her poem:

Children Learn What They Live

If a child lives with criticism,
  He learns to condemn.

If a child lives with hostility,
  He learns to fight.

If a child lives with ridicule,
  He learns to be shy.

If a child lives with shame,
  He learns to feel guilty.

If a child lives with tolerance,
  He learns to be patient.

If a child lives with encouragement,
	He learns confidence.

If a child lives with praise,
	He learns to appreciate.

If a child lives with fairness,
	He learns justice.

If a child lives with security,
	He learns to have faith.

If a child lives with approval,
	He learns to like himself.

If a child lives with acceptance and friendship,
	He learns to find love in the world.

If your child sees you love your neighbor—he will most likely love his. If he sees you love Jesus—he will most likely do the same. Jesus said He did what He saw His Father do.

We have spent some time discussing how to correct and train our children. We have observed that the experience of older women is valuable when they teach the Word of God. But all of the above information may be totally useless to the type of person who needs to hear what not to do, which in return will reveal what can be done. Therefore, the following "hints" were compiled by the Houston, Texas, Police Department for such a person.

Helpful Hints on How to Bring up Delinquents

1. Begin with infancy to give the child everything he wants. He will then grow up to believe the world owes him a living.

2. When he picks up bad words, laugh at him. He will think he is cute. It will encourage him to think up "cuter" words and phrases that will blow off the top of your head later.

3. Never give him any spiritual training. When he is 21 let him decide for himself what he wants to be. (Don't be surprised if he decides to be "nothing.")

4. Avoid the word "Wrong." It might develop a guilt complex. A few years later, when he is arrested for stealing a car, he will feel that society is against him and that he is being persecuted.

5. Pick up after him. This means wet towels, books, shoes, and clothing. Do everything for him. He will then become experienced in evading responsibility and incapable of finishing any task.

6. Let him see everything, hear everything and read everything smutty he can get his hands on. Make sure the silverware and drinking glasses are sterilized but let his mind feed on garbage.

7. If you have a serious conflict in opinion with your spouse, fight it out in front of the children. It's good for the youngsters to view their parents as human beings who express themselves freely and openly. Later, if you get divorced, they'll know what caused it.

8. Give your children all the spending money they want. After all, one of the reasons you have worked so hard all your life is to make life easier for your children. Why should they have it as rough as you?

9. Satisfy his every craving for food, drink, and comfort. See that his every desire is satisfied. Denial might lead to harmful frustration.

10. Take your child's part against neighbors, teachers, and friends. This will prepare you to take his part against the police.

11. When he gets into serious trouble, apologize for yourself by saying, "I can't understand why he turned out like this. We gave him everything."

12. Prepare for a life of grief. You are apt to have it.

Chapter 5

LESBIAN SPIRIT ON THE PROWL

This title could very easily be rewritten by saying "Lesbian Spirit or Women's Free Liberation on the Prowl" and be just as accurate. Have you ever asked yourself the questions, "What is the lesbian spirit?" or, "What does Women's Free Liberation mean?" If you have taken the time to ask these questions, then you surely must be aware of the similarity they portray.

Where does the word *lesbian* come from and what does it denote in our society? The term is popularly used to connote female homosexuality since it was in the Aegean Island of Lesbos that the Greek poetess, Sappho, in the earlier half of the sixth century B.C., made herself the leader of a group of women whose mutual relations were characterized by strong homosexual feelings.

Homosexual attraction among females is not by any means always associated with homosexual practices. These practices, where they occur, include various activities such as "tribadism" (a form of masturbation, meaning "to rub"), which is the most common method; mouth-genital contact; and the use of a phallus.

Homosexual practices in our society are believed to occur much less widely among women than among men, and seem never to have been thought to constitute so grave a danger to society. But this view is mistaken—homosexual love, according to Ignace Lepp in her book *The Psychology of Loving,* indicates it to be even more frequent among women than among men, although the fixation among men is generally much less exclusive in character.

Biblical references to female homosexuality are found in both the Old and New Testaments. The Jews, while strongly disapproving of it, seem to have considered its practicing as less of a moral or social evil than male homosexuality.

Satan himself has grabbed hold of God's creation, "man," and distorted his thinking to the degree that homosexuality in itself has become an acceptable part of our society. Today lesbianism is practiced by small groups of women as a "cult" or religion.

The Apostle Paul warned his readers concerning the devil and how he goes throughout the whole earth devouring all he can, including man's thinking.

Today's society is beginning to view homosexuality as less of a "sin" being committed by a certain group of people; but on the contrary, the homosexual is being viewed today more as a third type of person in himself—a people different from the traditional heterosexual male and female, with all of the rights to express their emotional love and affection in the way they see fit.

The lesbian spirit reaches out to possess and influence young women in two basic and sly approaches; one through the sexual deviated acts, and the other through adornment (I Peter 3:3-4). It is through the attitude toward men and outward apparel (mannish), that "Women's Free Liberation" reveals its lesbian spirit.

The Bible tells us all forms of incest are forbidden under the law. *Incest* is sexual intercourse between close relations, such as brother and sister, or father and daughter, or mother and son, uncles and nieces, or man with man, woman with woman (homosexuality), and various sexual acts with animals on man's behalf. The Word of God strongly emphasizes such acts as being an abomination to death (Leviticus 20:11-16). It was such practices as these, along with pride and riches, and not helping the poor that brought the wrath of God upon the two cities of Sodom and Gomorrah (Genesis 19:1-16). Even today the words Sodomy and Sodomite refer to certain deviate acts. Young women, the practice of wearing the garments of the opposite sex and pretending to be such is also an abomination to God (Deuteronomy 22:5).

Sexual deviate practices are always associated with idolatry and rebellion against God in the Scriptures. Romans 1:18-32 reveals this alliance and its fearful results very plain.

For the wrath of God is revealed from heaven against all ungodliness and unrighteousness of men . . . when they knew God, they glorified him not as God, neither were thankful, but became vain in their imaginations and their foolish hearts were darkened . . . they changed the glory of the uncorruptible God into an image . . . wherefore God gave them up to uncleanness (that is impurity, moral defilement, such as is specified in vs. 26, 27. Gross immorality usually accompanies idolatry and was anciently consecrated as a part of religion) **through the lusts of their own hearts** (or, "in the lusts"; this refers to the moral condition in which they were already when God left them to the consequences of their depraved inclinations and desires) **to dishonor their own bodies between themselves. God gave them up to vile affections; for even their women did change the natural use into that which is against nature and likewise the men, leaving the natural use of the woman, burned in their lust one toward another; men with men working that which is unseemly, and receiving in**

themselves (in their bodies and in their emotions) **the recompense** (payment) **of their error which was meet.**

This means that oral sex is wrong also, even in marriage. Oral sex is unclean and an abomination to God. I have worked with many couples, even divorced young people, whose marriage is breaking up or has broken up because of oral sex.

Oral sex means to use lips or mouth area for gratification, rather than natural intercourse. This kind of pervertedness causes the man to become a homosexual and the woman to become a lesbian, or bisexual. This type of gratification works on the nerves and the sensual rather than God's love for each other. (Animals don't have the higher degree of love [God's love] yet they have sensation.) After a while the wife isn't satisfied nor is the husband. The wife gets sick of this kind of sex and does not believe the husband loves her. This way of love-making is an unclean spirit. God's Word tells us to come out from the unclean ways.

Paul in Romans Chapter One is referring to the physical and emotional changes that occur among those who practice homosexuality. Men become effeminate, sometimes suffering voice changes and other physical changes, becoming emotionally disturbed and sometimes incapable of a normal act of heterosexual intercourse. Women tend to become masculine as a result of such practice.

Young women, God does not desert us or leave us alone to struggle with our own problems. The sin of homosexuality is curable. The Apostle Paul mentions this in I Corinthians 6:9-11. He tells us, v. 9, **"Know ye not?"** This type of question expects a positive answer. It could be restated as, "Surely you know," in relationship to the thought, "Have you departed so far from the teaching of the gospel and the principles of righteousness that you do not realize that there is no place in the Kingdom of God for anyone guilty of these things?" **"that the unrighteous shall not inherit the kingdom of God?"** (The unjust who seek to benefit themselves at the expense of their brethren will not enter into God's Kingdom. Their greedy, grasping, selfish character is altogether out of harmony with the selfless, humble love that characterizes the inhabitants of paradise.) **"Be not deceived"**; (Sin blinds its devotees so that often they do not seem to realize they are doing wrong or, if they do, their senses are so dulled and benumbed by indulgence in evil that they seem unaware of the danger that threatens them.) **"Neither fornicators, nor idolaters,"** (among heathen people licentiousness is usually connected with idol worship. It centers in the sexual abuse of the human body, and those who practice it may be said to make an idol of the means by which their lust is gratified.) **"nor adulterers, nor effeminate,"** (meaning basically "soft of nature" or "delicate" or "tender" when used in relationship to sensual vice.) **"nor abusers of themselves with mankind,"** (another phrase describing homosexuals. He who lives a life of slavery to the sins of the flesh not only forfeits his own chance of a share in the glorious inheritance of the saints but passes on to his offsprings a legacy of weakness, both physical and spiritual.) v. 10: **"nor thieves, nor covetous, nor drunkards, nor revilers (slanderers), nor extortioners, shall inherit the kingdom of God."** v. 11: **"and such were some of you"**; (Prior to conversion the Corinthians had indulged in the vices here mentioned, and now they were free from them.)

Young women, this is your freedom! Freedom to know Satan's hold upon you can be broken. Homosexuality is a sin that can be healed—*not a new race that must be accepted, but a wrong that must be corrected.* The question is asked, "How can it be corrected?" Paul's answer is in verse 11, **"but ye are washed, but ye are sanctified, but ye are justified in the name of the Lord Jesus, and by the**

Spirit of our God." (When Jesus' love satisfies, one is satisfied!)

The Father, looking upon the converted sinner, sees the beautiful garment of Christ's righteousness with which the repentant one has been covered, and not the sin-stained rags of the sinner's own corrupt life. This amazing transaction has been made possible by the sacrificial death of Jesus. In view of the fact that the Holy Spirit works this transformation from sin to righteousness, believers are under moral obligation to live lives of continual surrender to the Lord's will at all times.

I am asked by many women concerning themselves, "Why am I a lesbian? How did it happen to me? Can you help me?"

My answer often to these young women is: Homosexuality and lesbian tendencies start at a young age in a little girl's life—before she reaches maturity. She is exposed to the wrong type of influences from her parents, friends and schools. She is not given the true perspective of what a young woman should be like, and therefore she patterns herself after the wrong model which society has presented to her. There is help for you.

The Apostle Paul said, "And such were some of you" (I Corinthians 6:11). These words are telling you that if you want freedom from homosexuality, you can have it by giving yourself to Jesus Christ and the Holy Spirit. It takes much laboring in prayer and in the Word. The period of time it takes is as varied as the case.

There is no Scripture to support the notion that homosexuals have always been so *by nature*. The overwhelming evidence is that homosexuality is learned, not inborn. Even if we accept the idea that some people are born straight and some are born homosexual, one big problem remains: how do you decide which you are? Purely by subjective feelings? To build a system of theology on personal feeling rather than Scriptural fact is the quickest road to error.

The Apostle Paul himself called homosexuality an "error" (Romans 1:2-27). If homosexuality can be learned then it can also be "unlearned"—this is the stage you are at now, the beginning of unlearning, or we might say being *delivered*. One of the first signs of the believer is "to cast out devils."

Young women, be careful in the raising of your children that you will not raise them according to the ways of homosexuality. "Women's Free Liberation" is one of these ways. All women involved in "Women's Free Liberation" are **not** lesbians and may never be, but I am saying the devil is using this type of error to distort the woman's perspective of what the true role of a woman should be. Any woman experiencing less than the true role of a humble woman can never and will never experience complete contentment with herself, her husband, or her children. Believe it or not, it has gotten into the church through disguise.

A real and complete woman is a woman who is totally free in the Lord. She will follow and practice the principles outlined in the Word of God concerning what she as a complete woman should be. She will desire her husband to be the priest and leader of the home. She will depend upon him to support her both physically and spiritually and protect her at all times. (This is not saying she cannot help to support during times of crisis both physically and spiritually, but it is saying the husband should have the final and last word and responsibility in the matter.) This type of leadership from the husband is liberty in itself to the God-fearing woman. These kind of men are also hard to find. Any woman who would not want a strong man to watch over her is not ready for marriage.

A woman of God will not strive to be equal with man

or desire to be over him. Such action is the guidance of the lesbian spirit, and is the objective of "Women's Free Liberation." The product or results which this lesbian spirit brings is the distortion and destruction of good marriages and friendships, and is against the Bible teaching of young women raising their children according to God's way.

We must remember our society and man's teaching, which we have placed so much trust in, is without God's direction. This has played a real trick on the women of today, by taking away their real liberty and giving them bondage.

Our society, a society which experiences three divorces out of every four marriages, is placing a tremendous burden upon the women of today. More today than in any other time in history, women are raising other women's children who are frustrated and unwilling to be loved by them. The method which women today are seeking to use to solve this perplexity they call "Women's Free Liberation," but this is not the answer. God has a better answer. The answer is obtainable, and it is possible with God's help to redirect these misguided women back to the original plan which God had designed for them.

This demands your acceptance of the responsibility to be aware of the bad influences which have guided you or could lead you astray from God's ideal plan for you.

It has been my own experience out of every five girls between the ages of seven to seventeen who have come to live in our home, three of them have practiced lesbianism in one way or another. So I have felt compelled to search for the reason. What experiences did they have in common? The answer was soon to be found: school. The public high schools, whether realized or not, are teaching and fostering lesbianism and homosexuality within their educational curriculum.

Take the P.E. teacher named Lori. She was a confessed

lesbian for seven years. Five of those seven years she lived with another woman, having sex, and the whole lesbian trip. She had this competitive spirit against men. She could not bear it unless she won. She finally found Jesus but could not seem to give it all up for Him. She did, however, comment to me one day, "Many women P.E. teachers are lesbians." She shared that a good percentage of young girls in sports are turning to lesbianism. "They talk openly about it. They speak as if it is a normal thing rather than something being evil."

One high school I know of in particular offers home economics where they teach boys to cook, auto mechanics and carpentry for girls, and co-educational P.E. classes with sharing showers and bathrooms. As far as dress standards are concerned girls may wear boys' clothing and the same short haircuts as the boys. One of the objectives is to instill within the girls a positive mental attitude which will foster individuality and complete independence from the male and thus assume the male's job, position, authority and leadership role. Girls are taking so much of the leadership role upon themselves they even initiate their own telephone calls to ask boys for dates. When the girls do succeed in obtaining a date, they do not give the young man an opportunity to even open the car door. This causes other courtesies, as well, to disappear. Politeness seems to be of no value in today's society.

Young women, slow down! Do not lose your true freedom by fighting for equality. You should remember to take the lowly and meek position, always giving honor, preferring one another, especially to the young men at an early age and, therefore, later you will treat men and your husbands in the same meek manner. They in turn will respect you as young women of God.

It is time we women begin instilling within our men what they can be and should be instead of trying to destroy them. They should be men of God, strong leaders over women.

I have young girls come to me saying, "Show me an example of a man that is a man of God that I can look up to." They complain they cannot find such a man of God who could fill the role of the priest in the home. But I tell them the problem lies with us—it is our fault. If we would get our lives straightened out and back to the Word of God, the young men would be compelled to treat us as women of God, and thus once again they would accept the responsibility as God-fearing young men and the priestly role of the home would again be restored.

I love men because God created them; whether they be husband, brother, or son.

Young women, respect men according to the position God put them in. Therefore, it is your responsibility to add to and build up your young man, instead of tearing down and pulling away. We need our men because they are vital, they are all we have. Pray continually the words of the psalmist: "Search me, O God, and know my heart: try me, and know my thoughts. And see if there be any wicked way in me, and lead me in the way everlasting" (Psalm 139:23-24).

Lev. 20:11 And the man that lieth with his father's wife hath uncovered his father's nakedness: both of them shall surely be put to death; their blood shall be upon them.

:12 And if a man lie with his daughter in law, both of them shall surely be put to death: they have wrought confusion; their blood shall be upon them.

:13 If a man also lie with mankind, as he lieth with a woman, both of them have committed an abomination: they shall surely be put to death; their blood shall be upon them.

:14 And if a man take a wife and her mother, it is wickedness: they shall be burnt with fire, both he and they; that there be no wickedness among you.

:15 And if a man lie with a beast, he shall surely be put to death: and ye shall slay the beast.

:16 And if a woman approach unto any beast, and lie down thereto, thou shalt kill the woman, and the beast: they shall surely be put to death; their blood shall be upon them.

Gen. 19:1 And there came two angels to Sodom at even; and Lot sat in the gate of Sodom: and Lot seeing them rose up to meet them; and he bowed himself with his face toward the ground.

:2 And he said, Behold now, my lords, turn in, I pray you, into your servant's house, and tarry all night, and wash your feet, and ye shall rise up early, and go on your ways. And they said, Nay; but we will abide in the street all night.

:3 And he pressed upon them greatly; and they turned in unto him, and entered into his house; and he made them a feast, and did bake unleavened bread, and they did eat.

:4 But before they lay down, the men of the city, even the men of Sodom, compassed the house round, both old and young, all the people from every quarter:

:5 And they called unto Lot, and said unto him, Where are the men which came in to thee this night? Bring them out unto us, that we may know them.

:6 And Lot went out at the door unto them, and shut the door after him,

:7 And said, I pray you, brethren, do not so wickedly.

:8 Behold now, I have two daughters which have not known man; let me, I pray you, bring them out unto you, and do ye to them as is good in your eyes; only unto these men do nothing; for therefore came they under the shadow of my roof.

:9 And they said, Stand back. And they said again, This one fellow came in to sojourn, and he will needs be a judge; now will we deal worse with thee than with them. And they pressed sore upon the man, even Lot, and came near to break the door.

:10 But the men put forth their hand, and pulled Lot into the house to them, and shut to the door.

:11 And they smote the men that were at the door of the house with blindness, both small and great: so that they wearied themselves to find the door.

:12 And the men said unto Lot, Hast thou here any besides? son in law, and thy sons, and thy daughters, and whatsoever thou hast in the city, bring them out of this place:

:13 For we will destroy this place, because the cry of them is waxen great before the face of the LORD; and the LORD hath sent us to destroy it.

:14 And Lot went out, and spake unto his sons in law, which married his daughters, and said, Up, get you out of this place; for the LORD will destroy this city. But he seemed as one that mocked unto his sons in law.

:15 And when the morning arose, then the angels hastened Lot, saying, Arise, take thy wife, and thy two daughters, which are here; lest thou be consumed in the iniquity of the city.

:16 And while he lingered, the men laid hold upon his hand, and upon the hand of his wife, and upon the hand of his two daughters; the LORD being merciful unto him: and they brought him forth, and set him without the city.

Deut. 22:5 The woman shall not wear that which pertaineth unto a man, neither shall a man put on a woman's garment: for all that do so are abomination unto the LORD thy God.

Rom. 1:2 (Which he had promised afore by his prophets in the holy scriptures,)

:3 Concerning his Son Jesus Christ our Lord, which was made of the seed of David according to the flesh;

:4 And declared to be the Son of God with power, according to the Spirit of holiness, by the resurrection from the dead:

:5 By whom we have received grace and apostleship, for obedience to the faith among all nations, for his name:

:6 Among whom are ye also the called of Jesus Christ:

:7 To all that be in Rome, beloved of God, called to be saints: Grace to you, and peace from God our Father, and the Lord Jesus Christ.

:8 First, I thank my God through Jesus Christ for you all, that your faith is spoken of throughout the whole world.

:9 For God is my witness, whom I serve with my spirit in the gospel of his Son, that without ceasing I make mention of you always in my prayers;

:10 Making request, if by any means now at length I might have a prosperous journey by the will of God to come unto you.

:11 For I long to see you, that I may impart unto you some spiritual gift, to the end ye may be established;

:12 That is, that I may be comforted together with you by the mutual faith both of you and me.

:13 Now I would not have you ignorant, brethren, that oftentimes I purposed to come unto you (but was let hitherto,) that I might have some fruit among you also, even as among other Gentiles.

:14 I am debtor both to the Greeks, and to the Barbarians; both to the wise, and to the unwise.

:15 So, as much as in me is, I am ready to preach the gospel to you that are at Rome also.

:16 For I am not ashamed of the gospel of Christ: for it is the power of God unto salvation to everyone that believeth; to the Jew first, and also to the Greek.

:17 For therein is the righteousness of God revealed from faith to faith: as it is written, The just shall live by faith.

:18 For the wrath of God is revealed from heaven against all ungodliness and unrighteousness of men, who hold the truth in unrighteousness;

:19 Because that which may be known of God is manifest in them; for God hath shewed it unto them.

:20 For the invisible things of him from the creation of the world are clearly seen, being understood by the things that are made, even his eternal power and Godhead; so that they are without excuse.

:21 Because that, when they knew God, they glorified him not as God, neither were thankful; but became vain in their imaginations, and their foolish heart was darkened.

:22 Professing themselves to be wise, they became fools,

:23 And changed the glory of the uncorruptible God into an image made like to corruptible man, and to birds, and fourfooted beasts, and creeping things.

:24 Wherefore God also gave them up to uncleanness through the lusts of their own hearts, to dishonor their own bodies between themselves:

:25 Who changed the truth of God into a lie, and worshipped and served the creature more than the Creator, who is blessed for ever. Amen.

:26 For this cause God gave them up unto vile affections: for even their women did change the natural use into that which is against nature;

:27 And likewise also the men, leaving the natural use of the woman, burned in their lust one toward another; men with men working that which is unseemly, and receiving in themselves that recompense of their error which was meet.

:28 And even as they did not like to retain God in their knowledge, God gave them over to a reprobate mind, to do those things which are not convenient;

:29 Being filled with all unrighteousness, fornication, wickedness, covetousness, maliciousness; full of envy, murder, debate, deceit, malignity; whisperers.

:30 Backbiters, haters of God, despiteful, proud, boasters, inventors of evil things, disobedient to parents,

:31 Without understanding, covenant-breakers, without natural affection, implacable, unmerciful:

:32 Who knowing the judgment of God, that they which commit such things are worthy of death, not only do the same, but have pleasure in them that do them.

NOTES

Chapter 6

VIRTUOUS WOMEN

The highest aim and concept which God has placed upon women is to pattern themselves according to the "virtuous woman." When I hear the term "virtuous woman," I think of strength, endurance, patience, love, and, above all, self-sacrificing. This is the challenge which God has given to women. To accomplish this challenge in its fullest sense is to stand upon the highest peak, shameless before God.

I feel saddened as I think of how Satan has distorted the true image and understanding of the "virtuous woman." Today, in our society, the characteristic of the "virtuous woman" seems to be something that we hide with shame and self-disgust. So many young women feel they will not be accepted by their peer group (both male and female), if they dare strive for virtues. Virtues in themselves today seem to carry a first impression of something weak, distant, and distasteful.

It must be remembered and understood, that such a woman as the virtuous woman is not a "powder puff" or just a member of the weaker sex which society dresses up and parades. She is a real person with feelings, needs, and hurts, and she possesses real responsibilities which, if carried out accordingly, will aid and benefit a virtuous man. Submission is one of the great attributes of such a woman, but the submission I am referring to must be drawn from her willingly by the components of both responsibility and love by a man of God. The type of submission she experiences never is bondage. She feels complete freedom because she is doing according to God's Law, therefore has peace in her heart.

The submissive woman should be looked upon as a capable person, willing and able to help her husband. She is worthwhile, and there is a responsible place for her.

The term "virtuous woman" means literally "a woman of power" or "a masculine woman," meaning that she is strong and hard-working, vigorous, and possesses excellent qualities. The Hebrew words may be interpreted as meaning "a woman of firm character!" And from those definitions I see no weaknesses which place her beneath man as being inferior.

The Word of God tells us, ". . . a prudent wife is from the Lord. The heart of her husband doth safely trust in her. . . . She will do him good and not evil all the days of her life. . . . She openeth her mouth with wisdom; and in her tongue is the law of kindness. She looketh well to the ways of her household, and eateth not the bread of idleness. Her children arise up, and call her blessed; her husband also, and he praiseth her. Many daughters have done virtuously, but thou excellest them all. . . . Whoso findeth a wife findeth a good thing, and obtaineth favor of the Lord" (Proverbs 19:14, 31:12, 26-29; 18:22).

This is the objective we are to strive to develop in our lives. We must seek to become the most perfect helpmate and wife a man can have. This responsibility is not totally ours alone, but is also the husbands'. If a husband fails to praise his wife for the good works she does and seems to have more interest in her as a provident housekeeper than as a companion, he causes her to become slack and careless, or hard and overbearing. We must not let this attitude overcome us even though our husbands treat us wrong. We must stand firm and keep our eyes upon the Lord. By such actions our husbands will see the value of the virtues in us.

The Word of God points out some of the responsibilities of the "virtuous woman" (Proverbs 31:13-28). Such a woman "seeketh wool, and flax, and worketh willingly with her hands" (v. 13). The *busy wife* takes a real pleasure in her efficiency. She goes out of her way to get materials to work on that will be of benefit to her family. She always looks out for the good of her family.

She will attempt to *save money* for the family by searching out and buying only the best at the lowest price possible. She may walk or ride for miles to obtain some advantage over nearer markets. There is also a great pleasure of bringing surprise items to the table to add happiness to the family circle (v. 14).

Such a woman is also a *good administrator.* She would appoint the day's work for her children at the same early hour, thus training them to be diligent as herself (v. 15). She is *capable of investing money* (v. 16). Her judgment can be regarded as important and sound. She can, with money earned, *make wise purchases* of land, and improve the land by clearing and cultivating it with her hands and planting a garden. Thus the original profit is put to work and grows and develops still more profit; yet no one suffers. Her gain is not another's loss. She is producing new wealth by her good management.

She is not a weakling; the true woman of God must be tough and sturdy even though she is often referred to as the delicate sex. She must be *willing and able to "girdeth her loins"* (v. 17), which means to tie up her dress a little higher off the ground than normally (or wear slacks) for the purpose of being free for active work. She learns to *love hard work* and considers it a pleasure, even the waxing of the floor, for it fosters within her feelings of usefulness, completeness and Christian pride. Her vigorous health and muscular strength are increased by her constant activity. She is *keen in mind,* "she perceiveth" (v. 18). By investigation she makes sure that her activities are profitable. She does not buy anything unless it is a good deal.

She is *willing to invest her time* by spending long hours working with her hands on the "spindle" (v. 19). Spindles are not much in use anymore, but if we have the time we can make rugs or mats by hand as I have seen many women do in Mexico and Jerusalem. Much pleasure can be derived from this type of activity.

She has a soft heart, *full of love and compassion* for the poor; "she stretcheth out her hand to the poor" (v. 20). No doubt some of her prosperity is due to her care for the poor and the consequent blessing and approval of God. "He that hath a bountiful eye shall be blessed; for he giveth of his bread to the poor" (Proverbs 22:9). We can help the poor by simply giving out of our kitchens. This is one of the concepts Pass It On Ministries follows.

She is *able to have peace in her mind,* she fears not what may befall her. She is prepared beforehand. She is like the ant; she prepares all summer long and gets things ready for winter. She is never caught without (v. 21). She *makes herself beautiful for* the household because she knows it is pleasing to her husband and children (v. 22).

She would *strive to lift the respect of her husband* in the community. She would desire her husband to be honored among his fellowmen. The good repute of her actions and the wealth she helped to create would do much to elevate her husband in the eyes of his friends (v. 23). She *helps him be the man of God* he should be and always encourages him and *finds only good in him.*

She is *a business woman;* "she maketh fine linen and

selleth it" (v. 24).

She *is of "strength and honor"* (v. 25). The capable wife and mother carries herself in the conscious dignity of proven ability. She laughs at the future for she has made ample provision for it.

She *speaks only wisdom and kindness* (v. 26). She *hates evil.* Her kindness is evident from her voice, whose soothing tones do much to keep quiet order in her household. She *is not lazy;* "she looketh well to the ways of her household" (v. 27).

Because she is sincere, honest and self-sacrificing, she reaps the greatest reward of all. Her children call her blessed and her husband praiseth her name (v. 28).

The making of a "virtuous woman" is not charm and beauty but complete sincerity and sacrifice. Charm and beauty in themselves are of little value. Beauty earns only the praise of the unthinking, but the only woman of true worth is the one who fears the Lord. She alone has true beauty and charm.

For men who cannot read the heart, the only sure way to estimate the quality of another is to study the fruit of the life as revealed in the works. In the gates of the city (v. 23), where judgments are made concerning all who live within the walls, the works of the "virtuous woman" speak for her, and she needs no other advocate. She will enjoy forever the sweet fruits of her unselfish toil and good example.

This is our guide to complete fulfillment and happiness. We must take hold of these characteristics and apply them to our own lives. We can become "virtuous women" of God. Do you see the value?

NINE VIRTUOUS WOMEN OF THE BIBLE
AFTER WHOM WE SHOULD PATTERN OUR LIVES

Deborah

She was the greatest judge in Israel, prophetess, deliverer, and mother. She judged, not as a princess by any civil authority conferred upon her, but as a prophetess, correcting abuses and redressing grievances. Her name literally means "bee." Of the judges whose exploits are recorded in the Book of Judges, she is the only one mentioned as possessing the prophetic gift. She is included here as one of the virtuous women due to her obedience to the Word of God. The Lord communicated to Deborah His purpose to destroy the enemies of Israel, and told her to send for a man named Barak, of the tribe of Naphtali, and make known to him the instructions which she had received. She accordingly adhered to the Lord's command (Judges 4:4-14; 5:1-15).

Dorcas

She was a woman of good works; she was raised from the dead through Peter's prayer of faith.

By some, Dorcas is regarded as a deaconess in the church at Joppa. If this is true, it may reflect the influence of Philip. He was one of the seven, and it is possible that he carried the organization of the church in Jerusalem into the churches he himself established. Thus, Dorcas may have had special care of the widows of the church. She is accredited with good works and almsdeeds, the latter meaning "mercy," especially as shown in giving alms; hence, "charity," or "benefaction." She was not content to be charitable as proxy like so many Christians of today, but she gave herself, as well as her possessions. We must be willing to do the same (Acts 9:36, 40-41).

Elizabeth

She was Zacharias' wife, and conceived John the Baptist out of a barren womb. She was the cousin of Mary, the mother of Jesus, and was filled with the Holy Spirit on Mary's visit.

Her name comes from the Hebrew word meaning "my God has sworn," or "my God is abundance."

Zacharias and Elizabeth belonged to that small group who eagerly studied the prophecies and looked for the coming of the Messiah. Among the Jews the term "righteous" had come to have a technical meaning and referred to those who strictly observed the ritual law and rabbinical traditions. It is obvious, however, that with Zacharias and Elizabeth righteousness was much more than an external conformity to the law. This is what we must be, more than what is called for. They were not mere legalists, but conscientious and exemplary in their fixed purpose to worship God "in spirit and in truth" (John 4:24; Luke 1:5-41).

Esther

Mordecai's cousin, Esther, was also King Ahasuerus' queen and an intercessor for Israel.

The name Esther closely resembles a modern Persian name meaning "star." This name is translated in Greek as "Esther." Mordecai's selection of a Persian name may have been due to a desire to conceal Esther's Jewish ancestry. She was willing to offer her life for the protection of her people. She is an example of what we as young women should strive to be (Esther 2:7; 7:1-8).

Hagar

It was an Egyptian handmaid to Sarah who conceived Ishmael by Abraham. God promised her many generations. The name Hagar is not an Egyptian name. Her original name is not given. The name Hagar means "flight" in

Arabic. It may have been given to her after her flight from her mistress. Abraham knew her with the consent of his wife, Sarah, and she bore him a son. Sarah became jealous of Hagar and restored her back to the status of a slave, as the civil law of that time permitted, and even took recourse to corporal punishment, as the Hebrew term "dealt hardly" implies. Therefore, Hagar left.

God recognized the difficult circumstances in which Hagar found herself, and for which she was not primarily to blame. Hagar honored the true God, and He would not abandon her in her extremity. Young women, we are to honor the same position. We should not let life's difficulties turn us away from God. We should stand fast and true. God had promised to multiply Abraham's seed, without limiting it to the offspring of Sarah. Therefore, He would abide by His promise to the very letter, but reserve the spiritual blessing for the seed originally intended by the promise, that is, Isaac (Genesis 16:1-16; 21:9-17; Galatians 4:20-23; Romans 9:7, 8).

Hannah

She was one of Elkanah's wives; conceived Samuel out of a barren womb; was a prayer warrior, and her only son of whom she conceived, she gave to the Lord. The name Hannah signifies "graciousness." She was the meeker of Elkanah's two wives. Peninnah, the other wife, used to tease and make fun of Hannah for being barren, but Hannah did not harden herself in sorrow and self-pity, nor grow sullen when spoken to by her husband, but manifested a commendable degree of self-control. She found refuge at the sanctuary. Hannah promised God if He would give her the gift of a son that she would train him and return him to the Lord. Hannah, at this point in her life, surrendered all and because of it God blessed her. Young women, we must do the same for our Lord (I Samuel 1:1-28; 2:1-11).

Mary

She was the mother of Jesus Christ our Lord; Joseph's wife, and one of many who was present on the day of Pentecost. She has been referred to as "the virgin" and the one "endowed with grace," which means the recipient of divine favor or grace (not the dispenser of it). Mary is nowhere called "blessed" except by Elizabeth and by an unnamed woman, and to the statement of the latter Jesus personally took exception. He always treated His mother with courtesy and consideration but never exalted her above others who heard and believed in Him. He did not call her "mother of God" or even "mother" but at the cross referred to her as "woman" a title of respect.

Mary was the kind of woman who would think things through and discover the true reason for the unusual experiences she received. Mary seems to have been not only a virtuous and devout maiden, but one of remarkable intelligence as well. Not only had she an unusual acquaintance with the Scriptures, but she also reflected upon the meaning of the various experiences that life brought her. Unlike Zacharias, who became afraid, Mary seems to have kept her presence of mind. Young women, we must attempt to expose ourselves to the Scriptures so we can become acquainted with them as Mary and, therefore, not become afraid when the Lord speaks to us (Luke 1:28; 1:42; 11: 27; Matthew 12:48, 49; John 19:26; Luke 2:19, 51; 1:12).

Mary Magdalene

She had seven demons cast out of her. She was the first to see Jesus after the resurrection. Mary Magdalene (probably "of Magdala," a town on the western shore of the Lake of Galilee) is listed among the women who accompanied Jesus on the second Galilean tour, and is mentioned in all four Gospels in connection with the death, burial, and resurrection of Jesus. The Gospels always mention Mary Magdalene first when her name is listed together with the names of other women. This testifies to her warm devotion to Jesus. Her gratitude was not merely emotional but intensely practical. The name "Mary" occurs frequently in the New Testament. It is derived from the Hebrew name translated "Miriam" in the Old Testament. Young women, we too should have such devotion to Jesus as Mary (Matthew 1:16; 15:39; 27:56, 61; 28:1; Mark 15:40, 47; 16:1, 9; Luke 7:38, 44; 8:1-3; 24:10; John 19:25).

Ruth

The love portrayed in the character of Ruth is of the purest, most unselfish, and extraordinary kind. Though a Moabitess, Ruth accepted Naomi's faith as her own, and was rewarded by marriage to a Jewish nobleman, Boas, by whom she became the ancestress of David and thus, eventually, of Christ our Lord and Saviour.

Ruth presents a most appealing picture of the blessings of the ideal home. The institution of the home came to us before the fall of man. The home was established by God himself on the sixth day of the week of creation. The home has become the special object of Satan's attacks.

The relationship of mother-in-law and daughter-in-law is a subject of amusement to many, but not so that of Ruth and her mother-in-law, Naomi. After a sojourn of ten years in the land of Moab, Naomi, whose husband and two sons had died, learned that a condition of plenty again prevailed in the land of Judah and decided to return. Ruth, with a devotion that speaks almost as much for Naomi as it does for Ruth herself, broke all ties of home and kindred to accompany her. With a last look at the fertile fields of her homeland, Moab, and with an impassioned outburst to Naomi, "thy people shall be my people, and thy God my God," she entered a strange land, united with God's true people, and became a worshiper of the God of heaven. Young women, if we could all become Ruths in our world today, we would receive true joy, peace, tranquility and contentment (Ruth 1:14-16; 2:21, 22; 4:13; Mark 2:27).

Prov. 31:11	The heart of her husband doth safely trust in her, so that he shall have no need of spoil.
:12	She will do him good and not evil, all the days of her life.
:26	She openeth her mouth with wisdom; and in her tongue is the law of kindness.
:27	She looketh well to the ways of her household, and eateth not the bread of idleness.
:28	Her children arise up, and call her blessed; her husband also, and he praiseth her.
:29	Many daughters have done virtuously, but thou excellest them all.
Prov. 18:22	Whoso findeth a wife findeth a good thing, and obtaineth favour of the LORD.
Prov. 31:13	She seeketh wool, and flax, and worketh willingly with her hands.
:14	She is like the merchants' ships; she bringeth her food from afar.
:15	She riseth also while it is yet night, and giveth meat to her household, and a portion to her maidens.
:16	She considereth a field, and buyeth it: with the fruit of her hands she planteth a vineyard.
:17	She girdeth her loins with strength, and strengtheneth her arms.
:18	She perceiveth that her merchandise is good: her candle goeth not out by night.
:19	She layeth her hands to the spindle, and her hands hold the distaff.
:20	She stretcheth out her hand to the poor, yea, she reacheth forth her hands to the needy.
:21	She is not afraid of the snow for her household: for all her household are clothed with scarlet.

:22 She maketh herself coverings of tapestry; her clothing is silk and purple.

:23 Her husband is known in the gates, when he sitteth among the elders of the land.

:24 She maketh fine linen, and selleth it; and delivereth girdles unto the merchant.

:25 Strength and honour are her clothing; and she shall rejoice in time to come.

22:9 He that hath a bountiful eye shall be blessed; for he giveth of his bread to the poor.

:26 Be not thou one of them that strike hands, or of them that are sureties for debts.

:27 If thou hast nothing to pay, why should he take away thy bed from under thee?

:28 Remove not the ancient landmark, which thy fathers have set.

:29 Seest thou a man diligent in his business? he shall stand before kings; he shall not stand before mean men.

NOTES

Chapter 7

TRY BEING LAST

It is hard to accept the notion that to be last is in reality to be first. In our society, which pushes, shoves, and cuts in front of others for the sole purpose of gaining an advantage, would never believe without much persuasion that the best position which would offer the greatest advantage is the position of being last.

Jesus repeated on various occasions the saying, "So the last shall be first, and the first last: for many be called, but few chosen" (Matthew 20:16, 19:30). These words were a warning to those who considered themselves certain of admission to the Kingdom of the Messiah on the basis that they were children of Abraham. Those who had the best chance to enter had not taken advantage of their opportunities but had slighted the advantages accorded them. The Gentiles, whom the Jews despised and considered unworthy and ineligible to enter the Kingdom, would, in many instances, more certainly obtain a place at the Messianic table for the simple reason that they had made better use of their opportunities than had the Jews.

Many, who like the rich young ruler, had every appearance of being first to enter heaven would actually be last. Matthew 19:30 forms a connecting link between the incident and subsequent discussion recorded in verses 23-29, and the parable of the laborers in the vineyard recorded in Chapter 20. Notice the same summary declaration is repeated at the close of that parable, verse 16, a parable that was told specifically to illustrate this great paradox of the Christian faith.

A few weeks after this occasion, during the course of His last day of teaching in the temple, Jesus declared to the chief priests and elders that publicans and harlots would enter the Kingdom of Heaven ahead of them (Matthew 21:31, 32). In fact, from all over the earth would come a host of humble, faithful ones worthy to "sit down in the Kingdom of God" (Luke 13:29), while the religious leaders of Israel would themselves be "thrust out" (v. 28). Another example which we must not forget is the parable of the rich man and Lazarus recorded in Luke 16:19-31. We must continually remember earthly success and popularity are based on altogether different standards from those by which God estimates a man's worth.

The Saviour gathered His disciples about Him and said to them, "If any man desire to be first, the same shall be last, and servant of all." There was in these words a solemnity and impressiveness which the disciples were far from comprehending. That which Christ discerned they could not see. Even though Christ gave them many examples, they did not understand the nature of Christ's Kingdom, and this ignorance was the apparent cause of their contention. But the real cause lay deeper. By explaining the nature of the Kingdom, Christ might for the time have quieted their strife; but this would not have touched the underlying cause. Even after they had received the fullest knowledge, any question of who comes first might have renewed the trouble. Thus disaster would have been brought to the church after Christ's departure.

The strife for the highest place was the outworking of

that same spirit which was the beginning of the great con-
troversy in the worlds above and which had brought Christ
from heaven to die. There rose up before Him a vision of
Lucifer, the "son of the morning," in glory surpassing all
the angels that surround the throne, and united in closest
ties to the Son of God. Lucifer had said, "I will be like the
most High" (Isaiah 14:12, 14); and the desire for self-
exaltation had brought strife into the heavenly courts, and
had banished a multitude of the hosts of God. Had Lucifer
really desired to be like the Most High, he would never
have deserted his appointed place in heaven; for the spirit
of the Most High is manifested in unselfish ministry. Lucifer desired God's power, but not His character. He sought
for himself the highest place, and every being who is moti-
vated by Satan's spirit, will do the same. Thus, alienation,
discord, and strife will be inevitable. Dominion becomes
the prize of the strongest. The kingdom of Satan is a kingdom of force; every individual regards every other as an
obstacle in the way of his own advancement, or a stepping
stone on which he himself may climb to a higher place.

If Lucifer would have chosen to be last, he could have
been even greater than he already was in heaven.

We must remember the last few words in Matthew
20:16: "but few chosen." The reason so few are chosen is
that they have already decided within themselves not to be
chosen. God's gift to us is: every person has free choice. If
we are to be chosen, we must ourselves decide and want to
be chosen, but that demands a sacrifice from us. We must
give our all, everything; we cannot hold on to anything like
the young rich ruler chose to do, which stole from him his
salvation.

I saw "Pop" going through the process of becoming
last. This process is hard. It seems when one of God's creatures who has gone astray attempts to come back, Lucifer
works on them just that much harder. In Pop's particular

case he had Jesus in his *head* but not in his *heart,* where Jesus belongs. He was a church-going man all his life, but he was not a Jesus-going man. Pop knew Christ and was a kind man, but he did not have Christ in his active life. There are many of us who desire to be good and attempt strongly to fulfill such a goal but are always found lacking because God is not governing our lives, or we are not permitting Him to.

Pop only assumed the position of being "last" two years before the Lord laid him to rest. Pop finally "let go and let God." He finally gave his all to the Lord. But Pop was a stubborn man, and the Lord had to place him on his deathbed twice before he would yield all to Him—his stubbornness, prejudice, and strong will, which were in themselves a form of idolatry.

Many of us, like Pop, must go to our deathbeds before our wills are yielded—the deathbeds of "dying to self." Put yourself in the last place. The Apostle Paul has said, "I must die daily to self." It is only after we have died to self that God can make us or raise us up to the position of being first. We must turn over our wills to God right now; it is never too late, God is calling us this very minute. Sure, some of us may be getting started late in life to be Christians, but if we yield our wills to God which we have established against Him by hanging on to our own desires, and we give Him our complete life, live for Him, He will cause us to be first in the Kingdom of Heaven.

The Lord used Pop in a very special way, the way many of us will never have the opportunity of being used. Pop had the glorious privilege to minister to people while in intensive care, both patients and workers, right up through the last minute before he left us to go through the glorious bright gates of the Kingdom of Heaven.

Satan works hard to rob from mankind his last chance and opportunity to turn his life over to God. Even in the hospitals today dying patients are so highly drugged their will and desire to live is pacified to the point to which they care not whether they live or die; in such a state, a death-bed repentance is improbable. This is one of Satan's tools which he uses to deprive man of salvation.

Young women, while you are yet young, yield your wills before God; "let go and let God" control your lives. This action will foster great strength in your marriage, and you will be able to minister to your husband, family, neighbors, community, and church with renewed and fresh zeal. We must let Jesus live His life through us. Remember, we have been bought with a price, and we do not own ourselves anymore. If we are willing to give all to Jesus, we will be looked upon by all as truly women of God. But the question is asked, "How do I give all to Jesus? I want Jesus to have His perfect will in my life. I want the position of being last so He can make me first in His beautiful Kingdom."

The answer is very simple, but it takes action on your part. You must be willing to give all. How do you do this? Bring it out in your cooking; make what your family wants to eat, not what you want to eat, and be willing to eat last. Be last to go to bed; make sure everyone else has been tucked away comfortably before you retire at night. Be willing to stand guard; be last to get your needs met; never even think of your own needs—let God worry about your needs; He will take care of you. The process of being last is not easy, but the rewards are overwhelming on earth and in Heaven.

You must ask yourself the questions: What position do I now hold? What position do I want to hold? What am I going to do about it? And then make your decision, for the time is now!

Most of all, make sure Jesus governs your life.

Matt. 20:1   For the kingdom of heaven is like unto a man that is an householder, which went out early in the morning to hire labourers into his vineyard.

:2   And when he had agreed with the labourers for a penny a day, he sent them into his vineyard.

:3   And he went out about the third hour, and saw others standing idle in the marketplace,

:4   And said unto them; Go ye also into the vineyard, and whatsoever is right, I will give you. And they went their way.

:5   Again he went out about the sixth and ninth hour, and did likewise.

:6   And about the eleventh hour he went out, and found others standing idle, and saith unto them, Why stand ye here all the day idle?

:7   They say unto him, Because no man hath hired us. He saith unto them, Go ye also into the vineyard; and whatsoever is right, that shall ye receive.

:8   So when even was come, the lord of the vineyard saith unto his steward, Call the labourers, and give them their hire, beginning from the last unto the first.

:9   And when they came that were hired about the eleventh hour, they received every man a penny.

:10   But when the first came, they supposed that they should have received more; and they likewise received every man a penny.

:11   And when they had received it, they murmured against the goodman of the house,

:12   Saying, These last have wrought but one hour, and thou hast made them equal unto us, which have borne the burden and heat of the day.

:13   But he answered one of them, and said, Friend, I do thee no wrong: didst not thou agree with me for a penny?

:14   Take that thine is, and go thy way: I will give unto this last, even as unto thee.

:15   Is it not lawful for me to do what I will with mine own? Is thine eye evil, because I am good?

:16   So the last shall be first, and the first last: for many be called, but few chosen.

19:23   Then said Jesus unto his disciples, Verily, I say unto you, That a rich man shall hardly enter into the kingdom of heaven.

:24 And again I say unto you, It is easier for a camel to go through the eye of a needle, than for a rich man to enter into the kingdom of God.

:25 When his disciples heard it, they were exceedingly amazed, saying, Who then can be saved?

:26 But Jesus beheld them, and said unto them, With men this is impossible; but with God all things are possible.

:27 Then answered Peter, and said unto him, Behold, we have forsaken all, and followed thee; what shall we have therefore?

:28 And Jesus said unto them, Verily I say unto you, that ye which have followed me, in the regeneration, when the Son of man shall sit in the throne of His glory, ye also shall sit upon twelve thrones, judging the twelve tribes of Israel.

:29 And every one that hath forsaken houses, or brethren, or sisters, or father, or mother, or wife, or children, or lands, for my name's sake, shall receive an hundredfold, and shall inherit everlasting life.

:30 But many that are first shall be last; and the last shall be first.

21:31 Whether of them twain did the will of his father? They said unto him, The first. Jesus saith unto them, Verily I say unto you, That the publicans and the harlots go into the kingdom of God before you.

:32 For John came unto you in the way of righteousness, and ye believed him not: but the publicans and the harlots believed him: and ye, when we had seen it, repented not afterward, that ye might believe him.

Luke 13:28 There shall be weeping and gnashing of teeth, when ye shall see Abraham and Isaac, and Jacob, and all the prophets, in the kingdom of God, and ye yourselves thrust out.

:29 And they shall come from the east, and from the west, and from the north, and from the south, and shall sit down in the kingdom of God.

16:19 There was a certain rich man, which was clothed in purple and fine linen, and fared sumptuously every day:

:20   And there was a certain beggar named Lazarus, which was laid at his gate, full of sores,

:21   And desiring to be fed with the crumbs which fell from the rich man's table: moreover the dogs came and licked his sores.

:22   And it came to pass, that the beggar died, and was carried by the angels into Abraham's bosom: the rich man also died and was buried;

:23   And in hell he lifted up his eyes, being in torments, and seeth Abraham afar off, and Lazarus in his bosom.

:24   And he cried and said, Father Abraham, have mercy on me, and send Lazarus, that he may dip the tip of his finger in water, and cool my tongue; for I am tormented in this flame.

:25   But Abraham said, Son, remember that thou in thy lifetime receivedst thy good things, and likewise Lazarus evil things: but now he is comforted, and thou art tormented.

:26   And beside all this, between us and you there is a great gulf fixed: so that they which would pass from hence to you cannot; neither can they pass to us, that would come from thence.

:27   Then he said, I pray thee therefore, father, that thou wouldest send him to my father's house:

:28   For I have five brethren; that he may testify unto them, lest they also come into this place of torment.

:29   Abraham saith unto him, They have Moses and the prophets; let them hear them.

:30   And he said, Nay, father Abraham: but if one went unto them from the dead, they will repent.

:31   And he said unto him, If they hear not Moses and the prophets, neither will they be persuaded, though one rose from the dead.

Isa. 14:12   How art thou fallen from heaven, O Lucifer, son of the morning! how art thou cut down to the ground, which didst weaken the nations!

:13   For thou hast said in thine heart, I will ascend into heaven, I will exalt my throne above these stars of God: I will sit also upon the mount of the congregation, in the sides of the north:

:14   I will ascend above the heights of the clouds; I will be like the most High.

NOTES

Chapter 8

BEING LEAST IS GREAT

Before you say this title is wrong, read what the following paragraph has to say. Jesus Christ always had some
way to make the seemingly obvious portray the opposite
meaning. For example, the highest form of love, the
"agape" love, which we read so often in the Word of God,
and hear proclaimed so frequently from the pulpit, is really not necessarily the highest form of love. The Greeks
themselves considered the "agape" love as an inborn love
which all mothers, if they were to be good mothers, must
have for their children. Surely a mother, they believed,
would love her own child. It was natural and demanded no
talent or sacrifice from the mother. It was not the type of
love which had to be developed and fostered. The Greeks
considered this love the lowest form of all. But Jesus,
through His example and application of this "agape" love,
transformed it in the Biblical sense to refer to the **highest**
form of all. Now look at this title again. Could it possibly
be right in saying, "to be the least is to be in reality the
greatest"? Think about it!

In the Gospel of Luke, Chapter 9, verses 46-48. we
witness the disciples struggling with a problem which they
couldn't seem to solve. They wanted to know which

among them should be greatest. Jesus, perceiving the thought of their heart, took a child and placed him to His side and said unto them, "Whosoever shall receive this child in my name receiveth me: and whosoever shall receive me receiveth him that sent me: for he that is least among you all, the same shall be great" (v. 48).

According to the definition of greatness set forth by Jesus, it is possible for all to be great. Matthew 5:5 portrays this beautifully: "Blessed are the meek, for they shall inherit the earth." As you can see, the "poor in spirit" are to receive the riches of the Kingdom of Heaven (Matthew 5:3); the "meek" are to "inherit the earth." It is certain that the "meek" do not now inherit the earth, but rather the proud. Nevertheless, in due time the kingdoms of this world will be given to the saints, to those who have learned the grace of humility (Daniel 7:27). Therefore, if you want to become the greatest, you must first become the least.

I've always had to learn the hard way. I was so impatient I could never seem to learn to wait for anything or anyone, including the Lord. But the Lord shook me and woke me up one day and taught me the greatest lesson I was ever to learn, which was "before honor is humility." I learned that to fill a high place before men, Heaven chooses the worker who, like John the Baptist, takes a lowly place before God. The most childlike follower is the most efficient in working for God. The heavenly intelligence can cooperate with him who is seeking not to exalt self, but to save souls. He who feels most deeply his need of divine aid will plead for it; and the Holy Spirit will give to him glimpses of Jesus that will strengthen and uplift the soul. From communion with Christ he will go forth to work for those who are perishing in their sins. He is anointed for his mission, and he succeeds where many of the learned and intellectually wise would fail.

But when young women or young men exalt themselves, feeling that they are a necessity for the success of God's great plan, the Lord causes them to be set aside, or strongly abases them.

It is truly great, as I have witnessed, to have the Lord wanting me to be the "least," but I must be careful in regard to human pride. When God puts me up front it really puts the fear of the Lord in me. We must remember not to become comfortable with just the front position. God does not always want us up front. Sometimes only a small amount of time is necessary and when God removes me, I retreat into my secret closet for communion again with Him (Matthew 6:6). The Lord reveals to me by the act of removing me from the front position that His work is not dependent upon me. The work does not stop because I was removed from it, but goes forward with even greater power.

As we look on the words of Jesus, we can see it was not enough for the disciples to be instructed as to the **nature of His Kingdom**. What they needed was **a change of heart** that would bring them into harmony with its principles. Calling a little child to Him, Jesus set him in the midst of them; then tenderly folding the little one in His arms He said, "Except ye be converted, and become as little children, ye shall not enter into the kingdom of heaven." The **simplicity**, the **self-forgetfulness**, and the **confiding love** of a little child are the attributes that Heaven values. These are the characteristics of real greatness.

Again Jesus explained to the disciples that His Kingdom is not characterized by earthly dignity and display. At the feet of Jesus all these distinctions are forgotten. The rich and the poor, the learned and the ignorant, meet together with no thought of the "Who's Who" club, or worldly preeminence. All meet as blood-bought souls, alike, dependent upon One who has redeemed them to God.

So, young women, we can praise God that we are not judged by what we have or how important we are in this

85

world, but by the substance within our inner being. The Lord raised me up in a ministry of being least. I myself had nothing, not even a name or a title, but the Lord insisted on pushing me forward—not in popularity or position, but in submission to work for Him. Therefore, Pop, my dear husband, who was so willing to sacrifice for the Lord and myself, opened our house before God. We never realized at that time we were to give up our bedroom for a prayer room off and on for the next ten years. The bedroom in our house has been filled time and again with every type of searching soul—from drug addicts to unmarried mothers. Pop and I found ourselves on a lowly mattress on the floor within our house, a place closer to God. I prefer to give up all—food, privacy, and comfort—just for the privilege to reach out and help these young people to God, who are in need; to be able to love them and guide them according to God's plan set for them. I want nothing in return, just the privilege to love them is enough.

When we are willing to be the least, in good time God will raise us up. I used to, and still do, pray three to five hours at one sitting, or rather knee-bending, calling unto the Lord to watch over and bless the hotlines and all the youth ministries in Orange County and the world. I called upon the Lord concerning His promise recorded in Matthew 6:6: "But thou, when thou prayest, enter into thy closet, and when thou hast shut thy door, pray to thy Father which is in secret; and thy Father which seeth in secret shall reward thee openly."

Prayer plays a very important role in the God-man relationship. Young women should be intercessors of prayer. A woman who is an intercessor of prayer is a woman who has chosen to be least in the Lord's work. But as the "agape" love which was least became the greatest, so is it with the intercessor of prayer; it is the greatest ministry of the body, the heartbeat itself. Many different types of ministries make up the body, but the intercessor of prayer is pumping down power from God and directing it through the veins to the many who are in the front-line positions of the body.

We should train ourselves to be this type of special power behind our husbands and pastors. All of us women can have this type of ministry anywhere if we are willing to yield to it. But we must be willing to become least for this is the foundation from which our greatness grows. Our first ministry is the home. The home is our Jerusalem, our husbands and children are the major concern. Only after our home is built firm in the Lord can we consider moving on to Judea, Samaria, or some other section of the world.

All women should be prayer warriors, praying for their husbands and children. The greatest influence a growing child can receive, which will direct the living of his life, will be from the example of a God-fearing parent, taking the position of being least.

No God-fearing man wants a woman to outshadow him, not because he has false pride, but because he knows it is contrary to God's perfect plan. This does not mean the woman can never take a leading role in the Lord's work. If her husband himself puts her, or rather agrees or gives his approval, in the leading role which God has anointed her to take, and informs the hearers of his decision concerning the matter, then it is acceptable for her to take such a position and he will still be maintaining his responsibility of the "priest" position of his household. For example, Pop would just be present when I spoke, or he would let them know that he approved of what I was doing.

In our society today we are perplexed with both divorced and widowed women. The latter are in the position where there is no choice to reunite with their husbands. The divorced woman is quite often in the position where she can reunite with her husband, but the question she must ask herself is whether she can reunite with her husband according to the Biblical principles. If such a position is not able to be reached, then an important decision must be made; the choice to follow her own lustful desires or to follow God's plan for her.

God has a plan for all women who are alone. I have been a widow for quite a few years now, and Jesus' answer to my life was to marry "Him," and become a prayer warrior for others and work for Him. By my willingness to do so and the example I portrayed by carrying out God's desire for me and my family, my children were encouraged and received strength to go forward. Whether widowed, or divorced, our children, if we have any, or other people's children, if they are able to see our example, should at least have one good parent or person after which to pattern their lives. It is always our responsibility, as children of God, to lead others in the right way (Matthew 5:19).

At first glance this seems hard, but Jesus Christ has promised we would not receive any temptation which we could not endure. The Lord has provided us a way. He will take our sex drives and motivate them in another direction. The Apostle Paul records for us in I Timothy 5:5, "Now she that is widowed indeed, and desolate, trusteth in God, and continueth in supplications and prayers night and day." The widow described does not assume an earnest deportment to win the sympathy and commendation of the church. From the beginning of her widowhood she has placed her future in the hands of God, knowing that His love will provide a solution to her problem. Paul, in this text, does imply that continual prayer should constitute the chief occupation of widows; he also states that God is their constant companion and their ready source of comfort (Read Isaiah 54:4-8). He'll be your husband and the Lord of hosts is His name.

We are to become prayer warriors for Him and place our lives in His hands. This is what I have done. I have given my Lord all of what I have and all of what I am. He in return has ministered unto me and through the strength of His ministry, Pass It On Ministries (helping the poor). This was my outlet and fulfillment the Lord had promised me.

The Apostle Paul in verse 10 describes some of the functions of the widow which raises her up before the Lord. She is to participate in such good works as bringing up her children, or other people's children, such as orphans. She is to lodge strangers and offer them a helping hand when in need, and she is to wash the saints' feet. Eastern courtesy required that the feet of guests be washed. Special honor was presumably shown when the hostess herself performed this act. It also is an act of humility. She is expected to be engaged continually in all such good works before the Lord.

We are not to take this lightly. There were times in the beginning of this ministry that people gave me the worst piece of the pie; things nobody else wanted to do and people nobody else wanted to see or deal with. But because I was willing to do the work without pride or shame, God made this "least" job the "greatest." The promise and assurance God presents to us in His holy Word states, "Cast thy bread upon the waters: for thou shalt find it after many days" (Ecclesiastes 11:1). Also, what you do unto the least of them you have done it unto Jesus (Matthew 25).

The traditional interpretation of Ecclesiastes 11:1 is of exercising charity or kindness toward others, for which a reward will some day be received. The phrase "upon the waters" means literally "upon the faces of the waters." Whatever the figure of "bread" may refer to, the lesson is that of acting in a spirit of liberality and without expecting immediate returns.

I have many parents today who are very upset with me because their children prefer to come and live with me rather than to stay at home with them. These parents and their friends call me on the telephone periodically to call me all types of dirty names, but this I can take, for God has shown me the other side of the coin. Through my prayers I see lives changed, even the young people's parents. I see young people throwing off their old habits and reaching out for God and His perfect plan for them, which He had ordained from the beginning. This in itself makes the LEAST—GREAT!

Luke	9:46	Then there arose a reasoning among them, which of them should be greatest.
	:47	And Jesus, perceiving the thought of their heart, took a child, and set him by him,
	:48	And said unto them, Whosoever shall receive this child in my name, receiveth me: and whosoever shall receive me, receiveth him that sent me: for he that is least among you all, the same shall be great.
Matt.	5:3	Blessed are the poor in spirit: for theirs is the kingdom of heaven.
Dan.	7:27	And the kingdom and dominion, and the greatness of the kingdom under the whole heaven, shall be given to the people of the saints of the most High, whose kingdom is an everlasting kingdom, and all dominions shall serve and obey him.
Matt.	5:19	Whosoever therefore shall break one of these least commandments, and shall teach men so, he shall be called the least in the kingdom of heaven: but whosoever shall do and teach them, the same shall be called great in the kingdom of heaven.
Luke	7:44	And he turned to the woman, and said unto Simon, Seest thou this woman? I entered into thine house, thou gavest me no water for my feet: but she hath washed my feet with tears, and wiped them with the hairs of her head.

NOTES

Chapter 9

LOWEST SERVANT OF ALL

The concept of being the last, least, and lowest is the most important characteristic within the God-man relationship that permits us to be "safe to save."

After Christ had condescended to leave His high command, step down from an infinite height and assume humanity, He could have taken upon Himself any condition of humanity He might choose. But greatness and rank were nothing to Him, and He selected the lowest and most humble walk of life. The place of His birth was not a great palace in Jerusalem but a stable in Bethlehem, and on one side His parentage was poor, but God, the owner of the world was His Father.

No trace of luxury, ease, selfish gratification, or indulgence was brought into His life, but a continual round of self-denial and self-sacrifice. In accordance with His humble birth, He had apparently no greatness or riches in order that the humblest believer need not say Christ never knew the stress of pinching poverty. Had He possessed the resemblance of outward show, of riches, of grandeur, the poorest class of humanity would have shunned His society; therefore He chose the lowly condition of the far greater number of people. True faith is not to rest on evidence of sight. He was majestic and lovely. But when His ministry commenced, He was but little taller than the common size of men then living upon the earth. Had He come among men with noble, heavenly form, His outward appearance would have attracted the minds of people to Himself, and He would have been received without the exercise of faith.

The faith of men in Christ as the Messiah was not to rest on the evidence of sight, and they believed on Him not because of His personal attraction, but because of the excellence of character found in Him which never had been found, neither could be, in another.

While Lucifer counted it a thing to be grasped to be equal with God, Christ, the exalted One, "made himself of no reputation, and took upon Him the form of a servant, and was made in the likeness of men; and being found in fashion as a man, he humbled himself, and became obedient unto death, even the death of the cross" (Philippians 2:7-8).

Let's take a close look at these two texts:

Verse 7: "made himself of no reputation." Literally emptied himself. This emptying was voluntary (John 10:17-18). It was not possible for Christ to retain all the tokens of divinity and still accomplish the incarnation. "Form of a servant"; Paul is contrasting the form of God with the form of a servant and emphasizing the vast difference between the two estates. The word for "servant" in this text is commonly used for "slave" (Romans 1:1); so the apostle is saying that Christ emptied Himself and took on the essential attributes of a slave. As a slave's outstanding characteristic is that of rendering unquestioning obedience, so as a man, the Son undertook to render obedience to the Father (Hebrews 5:8). He grasped not at divine sovereignty but at service, which became the ruling passion of His life (Matthew 20:28).

Jesus' whole life was subordinate to the will of the

Father, as our lives should be. The life of Christ thus became the simple outworking of the will of God. How can any of us women who are so far inferior to Christ stand so much on our frail reputations that we find it difficult or impossible to yield our wills to the will of God?

When we share in the Spirit of Christ, when He dwells within us and we live the life of the Son of God, we will then be like Christ. "And was made"; rather (having become) in contrast with (being), or existing in the form of God (Philippians 2:6). "Likeness," that is resemblance. "In all things it behooved him to be made like unto his brethren" (Hebrews 2:17). He was a complete man, yet He was also divine. When men looked upon the incarnate Son, they saw one like unto themselves. "Men," the plural form is used, to emphasize that Jesus was to represent the whole human race, and not just an individual man.

Verse 8: "being found"; men discovered Him in human fashion. "Fashion," emphasizes the outward mode or form. To all outward appearances, Christ was a man and was so accounted by those with whom He lived on earth. "/ a man," Christ resembled a man. He had man's outward form, but He was more than that; He was God as well as man. "Humbled"; this is not the same as "emptied Himself" (Philippians 2:7), but is part of that emptying and shows one of the ways in which the self-emptying manifested itself. "And became," better read (having become), showing that the supreme act of self-humiliation consisted in Christ's voluntary submission to death. "Obedient"; Christ was totally obedient to God. He patterned His life in all ways after God's. "Unto death"; Jesus' obedience was rendered to the extent of laying down His life. It was humiliation indeed for God to become man; and then, being man, to die a shameful death on the cross.

Christ's obedience was the same nature as ours must

be. It was "in the flesh" (Romans 8:3) that Christ rendered this obedience. He was man, subject to the same desires to preserve His life as we are. He was tempted by Satan, but overcame Satan by the power of the Holy Spirit, even as we may do. He exercised no power in His own behalf that we may not employ.

"Death of the cross"; the emphasis is not only on the fact that Christ died, but on the kind of death. It was a death that involved intense shame as well as intense suffering. Crucifixion was reserved for slaves, non-Romans, and the lowest criminals. Paul knew well that if those to whom he wrote could come to grasp the astounding sacrifice made for them, there would be no place for selfishness in their lives. Now the cross was just before Christ; and His own disciples were so filled with self-seeking, the very principle of Satan's kingdom, that they could not enter into sympathy with their Lord, or even understand Him as He spoke of His humiliation for them.

Very tenderly, yet with solemn emphasis, Jesus sought to correct the evil. He showed what is the principle that bears sway in the Kingdom of Heaven, and in what true greatness consists, as estimated by the standard of the courts above. Those who were actuated by pride and love of distinction were thinking of themselves and of the rewards they were to have, rather than how they were to render back to God the gifts they had received. They would have no place in the Kingdom of Heaven, for they were identified with the ranks of Satan.

Young women, our goal is to be as Jesus was, with a humble and self-sacrificing nature.

In the Gospel of Luke, Chapter 1, verse 48, we are told God "regarded the low estate of his handmaiden; for, behold, from henceforth all generations shall call me blessed." The low estate referred to in this text can mean both "lowness" or "humiliation." The word refers to

Mary's low station in life, not to her spirit of humility. But even in the "low estate" Mary had "found favor with God," and this was to her of more value than all the treasures and all the honor and respect earth had to offer. Young women, although God is exalted high above heaven, He stoops low to touch the humble of earth. He looks graciously upon the poor in spirit and has promised to dwell with them (Isaiah 57:15).

We're living in a generation made up of young people who are taught not to serve, but to be served, especially is this so among the blacks. They are a prime example. At least some of them have been highly mistreated. Being a servant, at one time, was forced upon them. When freedom came they went to the extreme and refused to accept being a servant with joy. They haven't been taught by parents or grandparents to serve, but rather to get the biggest jobs. This generation is out of balance. It is tightly wrapped up in what is called racial freedom. This teaching is against God's perfect plan, for all humanity includes **all** races, if you happen to believe in races. I believe in only one race, the human race.

Don't lose heart, though. Satan may have won the battle concerning parents' training their children not to be servants or to be humble by advocating such actions as being weak and against freedom. But God won't let him win the war, for the only true freedom is in Jesus Christ, and that freedom was won two thousand years ago on a wooden cross at Golgotha (Matthew 27:33).

Parents today have slackened so severely in their responsibility of teaching and training their daughters that in latter years, when their daughters became young women, they were incapable of handling the normal domestic problems which adults are confronted with each day. Their parents thought it so much more important to go out and work to accumulate money for security in this world that

97

they permitted their children to virtually raise themselves without adequate parental supervision. This is why today I have young girls coming to my home to learn how to cook, take care of their babies, and to develop a sensitivity to be aware of other people's needs.

Unless young women are **taught** how to take responsibilities and be willing to assume the lowest role possible, they will never be able to find true freedom and happiness. If they continue to grow up with no responsibility, they will even be useless to their employers, for the way they handle themselves at home is a reflection of the way they will be in the business world. They must be taught how to serve their fellow man.

If we could measure a woman in the secular world in relationship to what she gives her boss in an honest day's work and what she gives her husband as a true wife, it would probably add up to about one-third or less of what she is capable of doing.

There is a difference between a female and a real woman. A real woman is a woman who possesses a servant's heart. Such a woman will continually reach out to serve where she is needed. Such a woman is blessed by God. Mary, as recorded in the Biblical records, was such a woman. God looked down and considered her lowliness as a handmaiden, and God let her bring forth the King and Saviour of the world.

Mary is also represented as the type of woman all of us should be like, the type of woman all God-fearing men look for, a girl with high virtues that saved her virginity for the day she was married and eternally carries within her mind the high objective of raising her children to be sons of God.

We must continually strive to be handmaidens. A handmaiden is a woman who is always on hand to serve. She is willing to serve with a smile on her face and not a complaint; she is a servant of servants.

In the Gospel of Luke, Chapter 10, verses 38-42, is recorded the story of two sisters named Mary and Martha. Martha was apparently the older of the two sisters and the one who administered the affairs of the home. She was the one who received Jesus into her house. Mary was more concerned with the spiritual and less with the material. Martha, in this story, "took thought" for the daily needs of the home (Matthew 6:25-34), whereas Mary sought "first the Kingdom of God and his righteousness" (Matthew 6:33). Martha, in this story, was rebuked by Jesus for complaining, not because she was doing work for the household; she chose to work instead of sitting at Jesus' feet. That was her choice, but she should have done so without complaining. We need a balance. We need to be alert and sensitive to our surroundings and make the correct choices between being a servant to man or a servant to Jesus.

I pray for more women with servants' hearts, with teachable spirits, and above all listening minds and listening hearts; not just listening ears (ears that just listen to spoken words), but ears that hear the meaning behind the spoken words. Such hearing demands action from us.

Above all things we need to remember lowliness of heart is the strength that gives victory to the followers of Christ; it is the token of their connection with the courts above. Do you have this strength?

John 10:17 Therefore doth my Father love me, because I lay down my life, that I might take it again.
    :18 No man taketh it from me, but I lay it down of myself. I have power to lay it down, and I have power to take it again. This commandment have I received of my Father.

Rom. 1:1	Paul, a servant of Jesus Christ, called to be an apostle, separated unto the gospel of God.
Heb. 5:8	Though he were a Son, yet learned he obedience by the things which he suffered.
Matt. 20:28	Even as the Son of man came not to be ministered unto, but to minister, and to give his life a ransom for many.
Phil. 2:6	Who, being in the form of God, thought it not robbery to be equal with God.
Rom. 8:3	For what the law could not do, in that it was weak through the flesh, God sending his own Son in the likeness of sinful flesh, and for sin, condemned sin in the flesh.
Isa. 57:15	For thus saith the high and lofty One that inhabiteth eternity, whose name is Holy; I dwell in the high and holy place, with him also that is of a contrite and humble spirit, to revive the spirit of the humble, and to revive the heart of the contrite ones.
· Matt. 27:33	And when they were come unto a place called Golgotha, that is to say, a place of a skull.
Luke 10:38	Now it came to pass, as they went, that he entered into a certain village: and a certain woman named Martha received him into her house.
:39	And she had a sister called Mary, which also sat at Jesus' feet, and heard his word.
:40	But Martha was cumbered about much serving, and came to him, and said, Lord, dost thou not care that my sister hath left me to serve alone? bid her therefore that she help me.
:41	And Jesus answered and said unto her, Martha, Martha, thou art careful and troubled about many things:
:42	But one thing is needful: and Mary hath chosen that good part, which shall not be taken away from her.
Matt. 6:25	Therefore I say unto you, Take no thought for your life, what ye shall eat, or what ye shall drink; nor yet for your body, what ye shall put on. Is not the life more than meat, and the body more than raiment?
:26	Behold the fowls of the air: for they sow not, neither do they reap, nor gather into barns; yet your heavenly Father feedeth them. Are ye not much better than they?
:27	Which of you by taking thought can add one cubit

unto his stature?

:28 And why take ye thought for raiment? Consider the lilies of the field, how they grow; they toil not, neither do they spin:

:29 And yet I say unto you, That even Solomon in all his glory was not arrayed like one of these.

:30 Wherefore, if God so clothe the grass of the field, which today is, and tomorrow is cast into the oven, shall he not much more clothe you, O ye of little faith?

:31 Therefore take no thought, saying, What shall we eat? or, What shall we drink? or, Wherewithal shall we be clothed?

:32 (For after all these things do the Gentiles seek:) for your heavenly Father knoweth that ye have need of all of these things.

:33 But seek ye first the kingdom of God, and his righteousness; and all these things shall be added unto you.

:34 Take therefore no thought for the morrow: for the morrow shall take thought for the things of itself. Sufficient unto the day is the evil thereof.

Chapter 10

WHAT IS REAL LIBERTY?

Throughout history man has always sought "liberty." The cry for freedom has been heard throughout every land. Whatever liberty is, it must be worth something for mankind has paid dearly for it, everything from money to their own lives, and Jesus Christ spoke highly of it and died to fulfill it.

Listen to some of the voices from the past, hear their urgency and their sincerity. Nathan Hale proudly stated before he was executed, "I only regret that I have but one life to lose for my country." He was fighting for liberty. William B. Travis wrote, "I call you for the sake of liberty, patriotism and everything dear to Americans to help us . . . I have made up my mind to hold out as long as I can and die like a soldier. We have made up our minds to victory or death." Also, Patrick Henry became famous for his words, "Give me liberty or give me death," which he spoke in 1775. We, too, are soldiers, in God's army.

Each one of these great men in history believed in the importance of "liberty," and reached out to fight for and obtain it. But Jesus Christ won and fulfilled the greatest "liberty" of all. He freed us to "liberty" by dying on a cross two thousand years ago. Jesus Christ, through His humility and great glory, fulfilled the requirements of the Law which in itself offers us eternal life and freedom, if we so choose. Jesus, throughout His ministry, offered freedom to all people. Some of the greatest words ever spoken came from our Lord while He was offering freedom to mankind. He said, "Take my yoke upon you, and learn of me; for I am meek and lowly in heart; and ye shall find rest unto your souls. For my yoke is easy, and my burden is light" (Matthew 11:29-30).

These two verses are telling us to submit to the discipline and training of the Lord's way of life. The words, **"take my yoke,"** are an encouraging cooperative effort. The purpose of a yoke was not to make the burdens of draft animals heavier, but lighter; not harder, but easier to bear. Thus the true meaning of the word "yoke" becomes clear. By "my yoke" Christ meant His way of life. The "yoke" of Christ is none other than the divine will as summed up in the law of God and magnified in the Sermon on the Mount (Matthew 5:17-22). The figure Christ here uses was not unfamiliar to His hearers, for the Rabbis also referred to the Torah (Deuteronomy 31:9) as a "yoke," not in the sense of its being a burden but rather a discipline, a way of life to which men were to submit, which in turn would set man free.

The word **"meek"** refers to bring "gentle," or "mild." Tame animals were said to be meek; they were submissive and harmless. One who is "meek" intends nothing but good toward others (Matthew 5:5). The word **"lowly"** refers to "humble." A person humble in his own estimation assigns himself a low position in comparison with others; he esteems others better than himself. Being "gentle" and "humble," Christ is a sympathetic teacher, and those who learn of Him will also be "gentle" and "humble." The words, **"find rest,"** refer to those who find the rest of which Jesus speaks will walk in "the old paths" and conform their lives to "the good way" of God's own choosing (Jeremiah 6:16). The word "easy" refers to being "fit for use," "good," "kindly," or "pleasant." By the phrase, "my burden is light," refers to those who truly love Christ. Such people will delight to do His will.

Those who take the "yoke" of submission to the Master, who "come" to "learn" in His school, will find the "rest" of the soul He has promised. The heavy burden of legal righteousness, of trying to gain salvation by means of merit supposedly earned by one's own works rather than secured through the merit of Christ, and the still heavier burden of sin itself, will all be rolled away.

This rolling away is the true freedom and the true liberty which the Apostle Paul speaks of concerning the Lord in II Corinthians 3:17: "Now the Lord is that Spirit; and where the Spirit of the Lord is, there is liberty." Paul in this text does not identify the second person of the godhead with the third but refers to their unity of purpose and operation. That such identity is not meant is evident from the next clause, "The Spirit of the Lord." In the New Testament the Holy Spirit is designated both as the Spirit of God and the Spirit of Christ (Romans 8:9).

The Apostle Paul is pointing out four functions or characteristics of the Spirit: *first,* the indwelling of Christ is accomplished by, and is equivalent to, the indwelling of the Spirit (John 14:16-20); *second,* the Spirit ministers the wisdom, truth, and righteousness of Christ (John 16: 10-14); *third,* the Spirit acts as Christ's agent in carrying forward the work of redemption and in making it vital and effective (John 7:37-39); and *fourth,* the fellowship of Christ is the fellowship of the Spirit (John 14:17-18).

The ministration of the Spirit means freedom from the ministration of the letter which, by itself alone, means bondage. To "walk in the Spirit" is to enjoy Christian liberty (Galatians 5:13-16; John 6:63). In and of itself the ministration of the "letter" engraved on tables of stone has no power whatever to convert sinners and to give liberty. It is only the Son of God who makes men "free indeed" (John 3:36).

The liberty of the Spirit is that of a new life which can always be allowed free and natural expression for the simple reason that when a man is born again his supreme desire is *that the will of God be made effective in him.* God's law written upon the heart (II Corinthians 3:3) frees him from all forms of external compulsion. He chooses to do right not because the "letter" of the law, but because now it is engraved in his heart, which now leads him to choose the right. The indwelling Spirit so controls his will and affections that he desires what is right and is free to follow the truth as it is in Jesus. He consents that the law is good and delights "in the law of God after the inward man" (Romans 7:22).

Liberty in Christ does not mean license to do as one pleases, unless one pleases to obey Christ in all things. There must be control. The less of it there is within, the more of it must be imposed from without. The man who is renewed in Christ Jesus can be safely trusted with full liberty because he will not abuse it by making it serve selfish objectives.

But what does *freedom* mean? Does it mean the liberty to do just as we please, when we please, without regard to anyone or anything? Just how free is freedom? How free is a train that is off its tracks? How free is an airliner without a navigational beam? Or a spacecraft without any connection to its ground control?

We held our breath a few years ago as Apollo XIII struggled back to earth after an explosion in its service module. What if the damaged ship should miss the slot where it must enter the earth's atmosphere? What if it should come in at too sharp an angle and burn up, or too flat an angle and skip off into space? If it had skipped the astronauts would have been *free* all right—free of all control. And they would have perished in the complete, uninhabited freedom of outer space!

Is there such a thing as absolute freedom? Anywhere? For anybody? Or do we just pretend there is?

Do the stars have absolute freedom? No. They are hemmed in by law. Their orbits were calculated by God when He created them and they travel in their orbits so precisely that our astronomers can calculate exactly where they were thousands of years ago and where they will be thousands of years from now. Do the oceans have absolute freedom? No, they are hemmed in, too.

What about people? Jesus told a story about a boy who thought he was hemmed in. He left home with the hilarity of a soul set free. But before the story ended, he was more enslaved than he had ever been at home. He decided he would be far more free as his father's hired hand! And so the prodigal son came home!

For some reason, it seems that every attempt to find freedom in the far country—every attempt to find freedom at the expense of conscience—ends the same way. With a famine at the end of it. But we keep on trying. And grumbling about the famine!

What is it about Christianity that turns so many young people away? Why does it seem so unattractive to them? You say it's too hard. It restricts you. It hems you in. It curbs your style and demands too much of a commitment. Well, does it?

It's true that Jesus did talk much about taking up your cross, denying yourself. And he told the rich young ruler to go and sell everything he had and give it to the poor. You get the idea that following Jesus is going to cost you something—maybe everything.

But strangely enough, right at the beginning of His

ministry, Jesus stood up in the meeting-house and told the people about His mission. And it's very interesting to see what He said it was. He said, "The Spirit of the Lord is upon me, because he hath anointed me to preach the gospel to the poor; he hath sent me to heal the broken-hearted, to preach deliverance to the captives, and recovering of sight to the blind, to - set - at - *liberty* them that are bruised, to preach the acceptable year of the Lord" (Luke 4:18, 19; Isaiah 61:1-3).

What do you think of that? He came to release the captives and free the downtrodden. Who could quarrel with a mission like that?

On another occasion He said, "You will know the truth, and the truth will set you free." And He said, "If the Son therefore shall make you free, ye shall be free indeed" (John 8:32, 36).

What do we have here—a contradiction? This same Jesus who talks about taking up your cross is talking about setting you free. He says that's why He came. Is this a contradiction?

Or could it be that in order to be free there must be some kind of control? Is it possible that the one who throws controls overboard and boasts about being free is in reality the one who is a slave? Could restriction be the only way to freedom? How free is one who is hooked on drugs, or alcohol, or gambling?

One summer a group brought back on their ship a large number of caged birds. About midway across the ocean, one restless bird escaped from his cage. In an ecstasy of freedom he flew away from the ship, out across the water. They watched him until he disappeared in the blue of the sky, then said, "That bird is lost."

After a few hours, to their surprise, they saw that bird, on heavy wing, coming toward the ship. Panting and breathless, the little feathered prodigal dropped upon the deck. How eagerly that bird, which had flown out over the water, had sought that ship again. That ship was not a prison. It was a home! And it was the only way across the ocean!

And so, like that little bird, we batter and bruise ourselves trying to get away from God. But will we find, in the end, that He is the only way across?

Make me a captive, Lord, and then I shall be free. Is every excursion into the far country bringing us back to this? Why is it that we seldom find happiness in the far country? The dream of freedom, of having it our own way, is so attractive. Why doesn't it work? Why is the dream so lovely in the mind, and so disappointing in reality? Does the Father have some mysterious hold upon our hearts that keeps drawing us back? We start out for the far country. But something deep inside us stands up in the road and says, "No, this isn't the way."

The most bored and unhappy people are those who bulldoze their way through life saying, "I have a right to be happy." How often we have heard it. And how often we have been told by the experts that it is dangerous to repress a part of our personality. But I ask you, if it is harmful to the personality to repress the animal part of us, what about the higher impulses? What about the rest of us? What about the suppressed morality, the suppressed devotion, the suppressed spirituality? All of these are deep inside us, too!

The woman who says, "I have a right to live my own life," is probably living only a fragment of it, at the expense of the rest. There is no such thing as happiness when **conscience** goes one way and **conduct** goes the other. Happiness happens only when the whole self is going in the same direction. That's why the dream doesn't work. That's why the far country isn't as romantic as it has been pictured. The problem isn't the restraints and taboos of the

Father's House. It's something on the road saying, No. Somewhere along the road we run into the rest of ourselves!

You see, God isn't a killjoy. He isn't trying to cheat us out of something. He's trying to give us the real thing. Take the rich young ruler, for instance. Was Jesus trying to take away his riches when He told him to sell what he had and give it to the poor? Or was Jesus simply trying to tell him about a better investment? Jesus wasn't minimizing the importance of possessing. Rather, He was telling this young man how to get possessions that were really worth having, that would last an eternity. But he decided against it. What a tragedy!

God took a tremendous chance when He gave us the power of choice. He could have made us puppets. But no, He set us down in this rough and risky world with the awful power to choose our own way, to make or mar our own destiny. He took a chance on man!

It's a dangerous gift, this freedom—this right to choose. But God Himself will not tamper with it or take it away. For what would we be without the right to choose? Just robots.

Sometimes we wonder why God doesn't act when we think He should. Why does He let wars continue? Why does He let people keep on killing people? Why doesn't He step in? Why doesn't He do something? Why doesn't He stop them?

But when we ask these questions, we have to ask another. Why doesn't God stop US? We have rebelled, we have taken the wrong road—many times—right before His eyes. Why hasn't He stopped us? Why didn't He block our way?

When John was only four years old, he went away from his parents' vacation cottage. He didn't wander away. He *went* away. His mother and grandmother had gone for a walk in the woods and left him at the cottage. He felt abused. So he sulked and pouted. Then, with his chin up, he started out, determined to find them. His father was watching. He could have stopped him. He was stronger than the boy. He knew the boy would get lost. By sheer force he could have stood in the path and held him back. Instead, he decided to follow him.

Down the rough road the little fellow tramped, with his father alongside him in the woods, hidden by the trees and the brush. Sometimes the boy stopped and looked back, not quite sure. But then his chin would go up and he would go on. He plodded on for almost a mile, until he became frightened and began to cry. When he turned back, his father stepped out of the woods, and said, "Well, John, are we going home now?"

The little fellow was not the least surprised to see his father. He only said, "John's lost." How like us! God has not made us puppets. He has made us persons, with all the risk of it. He won't impose His will upon us. He won't stand in the roadway and block our steps. But He'll follow along beside us in the shadows. And when we're ready to say, "John's lost," He'll be there waiting!

You have heard the cry for "liberty" throughout this whole chapter, but did you notice Jesus was the **only** answer for the solution? We must know Jesus, personally take hold of His hand and quit courting Him and marry up to Him. There's real liberty in knowing and living the Word of God. We can get to know Him through much prayer and meditation (I Corinthians 13; Galatians 5; Matthew 5; and Matthew 6).

Each of us should study the Word of God for ourselves; don't wait for some priest (Jesus Christ is our High Priest); accept Him and ask Him to govern your life, like Jacob of old who struggled with God, insisting on a blessing, and because of his insistence God blessed him above all others and changed his name from Jacob to Israel (meaning to be "governed by God"). Let Jesus rule your life, include Him in everything. Be another Israel.

We live in a time of sophisticated witchcraft, or, quite often called modern-day witchcraft, where the wrong and bad carry a first impression of being right and good. We are warned by God to be aware of these trappings and to stay away from them.

God created the world, and He alone is the true source of power. Satan did not create anything, yet he is the world's greatest counterfeit. All of his trappings have power but of a false nature; it is a power of death and bondage. But Jesus Christ has the power of life, love, knowledge and the spiritual gifts. Jesus is the One who will take you to that eternal life source, not Satan—he will only take you to eternal damnation.

I have received throughout the years into my home a large number of girls with many different types of problems, but the main problems center on seventeen areas in particular. You should become aware of these seventeen traps and guard against falling into them:

1. Horoscope (most popular)
2. Transcendental meditation
3. Philosophy of "self-realization"
4. Science of the mind
5. Yoga
6. Handwriting analysis
7. Extrasensory perception
8. False religions
9. Numerology
10. Drugs—pot, and also doctor prescribed drugs. Avoid continual reordering of these drugs: all of the zincs, stellazincs, liturium, muscle relaxers, valium, darvon, quads, pain pills, dexonol, diet pills, sleeping pills, and many more.

11. Wine and strong drinks
12. Exotic music
13. Lesbianism
14. Masturbation
15. Oral sex
16. Rebellion (same as sin of witchcraft)
17. Hypnosis

All of the above I consider as modern-day witchcraft, which we must constantly fight. The remaining twelve are Satan's trappings which are mentioned in the Old Testament, from which most of the above seventeen developed. They are as follows:

Enchantments: practices of magical arts (Exodus 7:11; Leviticus 19:26; Deuteronomy 18:10; 2 Chronicles 33:6; 2 Kings 17:17; 21:6; Isaiah 47:9, 12; Jeremiah 27:9; Daniel 1:20).

Witchcraft: practice of dealing with evil spirits (Exodus 22:18; Deuteronomy 18:10; 1 Samuel 15:23; 2 Chronicles 33:6; 2 Kings 9:22; Micah 5:12; Habakkuk 3:4; Galatians 5:19-21).

Sorcery: same as witchcraft (Isaiah 2:6; Daniel 2:27; 4:4; 5:7, 11; Micah 5:12).

Sooth-saying: same as witchcraft (Isaiah 2:6; Daniel 2:27; 4:7; 5:7, 11; Micah 5:12).

Wizardry: same as witchcraft. A wizard is a male and a witch is a female who practices witchcraft. Both were to be destroyed in Israel (Exodus 22:18; Leviticus 19:31; 20:6, 27; Deuteronomy 18:11; 1 Samuel 28:3, 9; 2 Kings 21:6; 23:24; 2 Chronicles 33:6; Isaiah 19:3).

Charm: to put a spell upon. Same as enchantment (Deuteronomy 18:11; Isaiah 19:3).

Magic: any pretended supernatural art or practice (Genesis 41:8, 24; Exodus 7:11, 22; 8:7, 18-19; Daniel 1:20; 2:2, 10, 27; 4:7, 9; 5:11; Acts 19:19).

The above seven traps are closely related to each other.

The "sorcerers" were charmers who professed to be able to produce magic spells. The word translated "magician" is the Egyptian equivalent of the Hebrew word translated "sorcerers." Magic was the object of much attention and study in Egypt, as texts on magic shows. It consisted to a large extent in charms that were thought to have power over men and beasts, especially over reptiles. That these men must have experienced actual results in their practice of magic is obvious from the fact that they were held in such high esteem through the centuries. It must therefore be assumed that they performed at least some of their wonders by the power of evil spirits, though many were no doubt only trickery, either way it was evil.

Divination: palm reading; the art of mystic insight or fortune telling (Numbers 22:7; 23:23; Deuteronomy 18: 10-14; 2 Kings 17:17; 1 Samuel 6:2; Jeremiah 14:14; 27:9; 29:8; Ezekiel 12:24; 13:6, 7, 23; 21:22-29; 22:28; Micah 3:7; Zechariah 10:2; Acts 16:16).

Necromancy: divination by means of pretended communication with the dead, it actually was done through demons (Deuteronomy 18:11; Isaiah 8:19; 1 Samuel 28; 1 Chronicles 10:13).

Astrology and star gazing: divination by stars (Isaiah 47:13; Jeremiah 10:2; Daniel 1:20; 2:2, 10; 4:7; 5:7-15).

The three traps of divination, necromancy and astrology are closely related. The literal meaning refers to a "consulter with the dead," or "one who inquires of an ('ob) or medium." An " 'ob" is the skin of a sheep or a goat usually used as a water bottle by men who supply villagers with water from a well or a spring. In Ugaritic literature recently recovered at Ras Shamra the word " 'ob" specifically means "departed spirit."

Prognostication: to foretell by indications, omens, signs, etc. (Isaiah 19:3).

Observing times: same as prognostication (Leviticus

19:26; Deuteronomy 18:10).

Prognostication and observing times are also closely related. Mostly referring to charms and incantations which tended to superstition and idolatry. It is astonishing to find that many today are still influenced by superstitious beliefs. Even reputable newspapers carry information on "lucky" and "unlucky" days. Men profess to be able to foretell the future by the position of the stars, and to advise what should or should not be done on certain days. Fortune tellers and spirit mediums flourish by the thousands, and millions are deceived by them. Some carry charms in their pockets or on their persons, nail horseshoes over their doors; others "knock on wood" lest evil befall them. Many will not begin or perform certain tasks on a Friday the 13th. The number 13 is thought to be unlucky. Some think a black cat an evil omen on a journey, and have been known to go back and begin their journey anew. Some refuse to walk under a ladder, and others again claim to cure certain sickness by throwing an object behind their back on a moonless night. Anciently such things were taken more seriously than they are today, and there was danger lest Israel delve further into the magic of the nations about them. Nevertheless, the judgments of God are just as severe today for anyone who is involved in this practice as it was in the time of Israel.

All of the above practices were and still are carried on in connection with demons called familiar spirits. All who forsook God and sought help from these demons were to be destroyed (Leviticus 19:31; 20:6).

Real liberty is being free from all of the above traps which Satan has set for us.

There are still churches blinded to the dangers within these traps. I know of some churches that mix the learning of magic along with the Word of God. But before we can help these churches we must clean our own heart and

115

make sure it is right before God.

In Illinois last year I went with my daughter, Betty Jean, to a well-known church, and to my astonishment they were having a "magic" show. I got up and started to walk out. On the way out I mentioned to one of the ushers that having a "magic" show in the church was wrong and he answered: "Oh, it's just for fun for the kids!" We cannot afford to play in Satan's ball field—it makes us vulnerable to destruction. No game is worth our salvation.

The road of a Christian is not easy. It demands much self-sacrifice. To reach the ideal which God desires for us we must first begin. It has been said, "Beginning in itself is being half done," but I say, "Finishing is completing the job!" We must actively strive to fulfill this ideal goal for our lives. How do we do this? By remembering that real *liberty* is coming back to the original plan of God and being willing to "LET GO AND LET GOD!"

Deut. 31:9   And Moses wrote this law, and delivered it unto the priests, the sons of Levi, which bear the ark of the covenant of the LORD, and unto all the elders of Israel.

Rom. 8:9   So then they that are in the flesh cannot please God.

John 14:16   And I will pray the Father, and he will give you another comforter, that he may abide with you for ever;

:17   Even the Spirit of truth; whom the world cannot receive, because it seeth him not, neither knoweth him; but ye know him; for he dwelleth with you, and shall be in you.

:18   I will not leave you comfortless; I will come to you.

:19   Yet a little while, and the world seeth me no more; but ye see me: because I live, ye shall live also.

:20   At that day ye shall know that I am in my Father, and ye in me, and I in you.

16:10   Of righteousness, because I go to my Father, and ye

see me no more:

:11 Of judgment, because the prince of this world is judged,

:12 I have yet many things to say unto you, but ye cannot bear them now.

:13 Howbeit when he, the Spirit of truth, is come, he will guide you into all truth; for he shall not speak of himself; but whatsoever he shall hear, that shall he speak: and he will shew you things to come.

:14 He shall glorify me: for he shall receive of mine, and shall shew it unto you.

John 3:36 He that believeth on the Son hath everlasting life: and he that believeth not the Son shall not see life; but the wrath of God abideth on him.

II Cor. 3:3 Forasmuch as ye are manifestly declared to be the epistle of Christ ministered by us, written not with ink, but with the Spirit of the living God; not in tables of stone, but in fleshy tables of the heart.

Isa. 61:1 The spirit of the Lord God is upon me; because the Lord hath anointed me to preach good tidings unto the meek; he hath sent me to bind up the brokenhearted, to proclaim liberty to the captives, and the opening of the prison to them that are bound;

:2 To proclaim the acceptable year of the Lord, and the day of vengeance of our God; to comfort all that mourn;

:3 To appoint unto them that mourn in Zion, to give unto them beauty for ashes, the oil of joy for mourning, the garment of praise for the spirit of heaviness; that they might be called trees of righteousness, the planting of the Lord, that he might be glorified.

I Cor. 13:1 Though I speak with the tongues of men and of angels, and have not charity, I am become as sounding brass, or a tinkling cymbal.

:2 And though I have the gift of prophecy, and understand all mysteries, and all knowledge; and though I have all faith, so that I could remove mountains, and have not charity, I am nothing.

:3 And though I bestow all my goods to feed the poor, and though I give my body to be burned, and have not charity, it profiteth me nothing.

:4   Charity suffereth long, and is kind; charity envieth not; charity vaunteth not itself, is not puffed up.

:5   Doth not behave itself unseemly, seeketh not her own, is not easily provoked, thinketh no evil;

:6   Rejoiceth not in iniquity, but rejoiceth in the truth;

:7   Beareth all things, believeth all things, hopeth all things, endureth all things.

:8   Charity never faileth: but whether there be prophecies, they shall fail; whether there be tongues, they shall cease; whether there be knowledge, it shall vanish away.

:9   For we know in part, and we prophesy in part.

:10   But when that which is perfect is come, then that which is in part shall be done away.

:11   When I was a child, I spake as a child, I understood as a child, I thought as a child: but when I became a man, I put away childish things.

:12   For now we see through a glass, darkly; but then face to face: now I know in part; but then shall I know even as also I am known.

:13   And now abideth faith, hope, charity, these three; but the greatest of these is charity.

Gal. 5:1   Stand fast therefore in the liberty wherewith Christ hath made us free, and be not entangled again with the yoke of bondage.

:2   Behold, I Paul say unto you, that if ye be circumcised, Christ shall profit you nothing.

:3   For I testify again to every man that is circumcised, that he is a debtor to do the whole law.

:4   Christ is become of no effect unto you, whosoever of you are justified by the law; ye are fallen from grace.

:5   For we through the Spirit wait for the hope of righteousness by faith.

:6   For in Jesus Christ neither circumcision availeth any thing, nor uncircumcision; but faith which worketh by love,

:7   Ye did run well; who did hinder you that ye should not obey the truth?

:8   This persuasion cometh not of him that calleth you.

:9   A little leaven leaveneth the whole lump.

:10   I have confidence in you through the Lord, that ye

will be none otherwise minded: but he that troubleth you shall bear his judgment, whosoever he be.

:11 And I, brethren, if I yet preach circumcision, why do I yet suffer persecution? then is the offence of the cross ceased.

:12 I would they were even cut off which trouble you.

:13 For, brethren, ye have been called unto liberty; only use not liberty for an occasion to the flesh, but by love serve one another.

:14 For all the law is fulfilled in one word, even in this; Thou shalt love thy neighbour as thyself.

:15 But if ye bite and devour one another, take heed that ye be not consumed one of another.

:16 This I say then, Walk in the Spirit, and ye shall not fulfill the lust of the flesh.

:17 For the flesh lusteth against the Spirit, and the Spirit against the flesh: and these are contrary the one to the other: so that ye cannot do the things that ye would.

:18 But if ye be led of the Spirit, ye are not under the law.

:19 Now the works of the flesh are manifest, which are these; Adultery, fornication, uncleanness, lasciviousness,

:20 Idolatry, witchcraft, hatred, variance, emulations, wrath, strife, seditions, heresies,

:21 Envyings, murders, drunkenness, revellings, and such like: of the which I tell you before, as I have also told you in time past, that they which do such things shall not inherit the kingdom of God.

:22 But the fruit of the Spirit is love, joy, peace, longsuffering, gentleness, goodness, faith,

:23 Meekness, temperance: against such there is no law.

:24 And they that are Christ's have crucified the flesh with the affections and lusts.

:25 If we live in the Spirit, let us also walk in the Spirit.

:26 Let us not be desirous of vain glory, provoking one another, envying one another.

Matt. 5:1 And seeing the multitudes, he went up into a mountain: and when he was set, his disciples came unto him:

:2 And he opened his mouth, and taught them, saying,

:3 Blessed are the poor in spirit: for theirs is the kingdom of heaven.

:4 Blessed are they that mourn: for they shall be comforted.

:5 Blessed are the meek: for they shall inherit the earth.

:6 Blessed are they which do hunger and thirst after righteousness: for they shall be filled.

:7 Blessed are the merciful: for they shall obtain mercy.

:8 Blessed are the pure in heart: for they shall see God.

:9 Blessed are the peacemakers: for they shall be called the children of God.

:10 Blessed are they which are persecuted for righteousness' sake: for theirs is the kingdom of heaven.

:11 Blessed are ye, when men shall revile you, and persecute you, and shall say all manner of evil against you falsely, for my sake.

:12 Rejoice, and be exceeding glad: for great is your reward in heaven: for so persecuted they the prophets which were before you.

:13 Ye are the salt of the earth: but if the salt have lost his savour, wherewith shall it be salted? it is thenceforth good for nothing, but to be cast out, and to be trodden under foot of men.

:14 Ye are the light of the world. A city that is set on an hill cannot be hid.

:15 Neither do men light a candle, and put it under a bushel, but on a candlestick; and it giveth light unto all that are in the house.

:16 Let your light so shine before men, that they may see your good works, and glorify your Father which is in heaven.

:17 Think not that I am come to destroy the law, or the prophets: I am not come to destroy, but to fulfill.

:18 For verily I say unto you. Till heaven and earth pass, one jot or one tittle shall in no wise pass from the law, till all be fulfilled.

:19 Whosoever therefore shall break one of these least commandments, and shall teach men so, he shall be called the least in the kingdom of heaven: but whosoever shall do and teach them, the same shall be called great in the kingdom of heaven.

:20 For I say unto you, That except your righteousness shall exceed the righteousness of the scribes and Pharisees, ye shall in no case enter into the kingdom of heaven.

:21 Ye have heard that it was said by them of old time, Thou shalt not kill; and whosoever shall kill shall be in danger of the judgment:

:22 But I say unto you, That whosoever is angry with his brother without a cause, shall be in danger of the judgment: and whosoever shall say to his brother, Raca, shall be in danger of the council: but whosoever shall say, Thou fool, shall be in danger of hell fire.

:23 Therefore, if thou bring thy gift to the altar, and there rememberest that thy brother hath ought against thee;

:24 Leave there thy gift before the altar, and go thy way; first be reconciled to thy brother, and then come and offer thy gift.

:25 Agree with thine adversary quickly, whist thou art in the way with him; lest at any time the adversary deliver thee to the judge, and the judge deliver thee to the officer, and thou be cast into prison.

:26 Verily I say unto thee, Thou shalt by no means come out thence, til thou hast paid the uttermost farthing.

:27 Ye have heard that it was said by them of old time, Thou shalt not commit adultery:

:28 But I say unto you, That whosoever looketh on a woman to lust after her, hath committed adultery with her already in his heart.

:29 And if thy right eye offend thee, pluck it out, and cast it from thee: for it is profitable for thee that one of thy members should perish, and not that thy whole body should be cast into hell.

:30 And if thy right hand offend thee, cut it off, and cast it from thee: for it is profitable for thee that one of thy members should perish, and not that thy whole body should be cast into hell.

:31 It hath been said, Whosoever shall put away his wife, let him give her a writing of divorcement:

:32   But I say unto you, That whosoever shall put away his wife, saving for the cause of fornication, causeth her to commit adultery: and whosoever shall marry her that is divorced committeth adultery.

:33   Again, ye have heard that it hath been said by them of old time, Thou shalt not forswear thyself, but shalt perform unto the Lord thine oaths:

:34   But I say unto you, Swear not at all; neither by heaven; for it is God's throne:

:35   Nor by the earth; for it is His footstool: neither by Jerusalem; for it is the city of the great King.

:36   Neither shalt thou swear by thy head, because thou canst not make one hair white or black.

:37   But let your communication be, Yea, yea; Nay, nay: for whatsoever is more than these, cometh of evil.

:38   Ye have heard that it has been said, An eye for an eye, and a tooth for a tooth:

:39   But I say unto you, That ye resist not evil: but whosoever shall smite thee on thy right cheek, turn to him the other also.

:40   And if any man will sue thee at the law, and take away thy coat, let him have thy cloak also.

:41   And whosoever shall compel thee to go a mile, go with him twain.

:42   Give to him that asketh thee, and from him that would borrow of thee turn not thou away.

:43   Ye have heard that it hath been said, Thou shalt love thy neighbour, and hate thine enemy.

:44   But I say unto you, Love your enemies, bless them that curse you, do good to them that hate you, and pray for them which despitefully use you, and persecute you;

:45   That ye may be the children of your Father which is in heaven: for he maketh his sun to rise on the evil and on the good, and sendeth rain on the just and on the unjust.

:46   For if ye love them which love you, what reward have ye? Do not even the publicans the same?

:47   And if ye salute your brethren only, what do ye more than others? do not even the publicans so?

:48   Be ye therefore perfect, even as your Father which is in heaven is perfect.

Matt. 6:1   Take heed that ye do not your alms before men, to be seen of them: otherwise ye have no reward of your Father which is in heaven.

:2   Therefore when thou doest thine alms, do not sound a trumpet before thee, as the hypocrites do in the synagogues and in the streets, that they may have glory of men. Verily I say unto you, They have their reward.

:3   But when thou doest alms, let not thy left hand know what thy right hand doeth:

:4   That thine alms may be in secret: and thy Father, which seeth in secret himself shall reward thee openly.

:5   And when thou prayest, thou shalt not be as the hypocrites are: for they love to pray standing in the synagogues and in the corners of the streets, that they may be seen of men. Verily I say unto you, They have their reward.

:6   But thou, when thou prayest, enter into thy closet, and when thou hast shut thy door, pray to thy Father which is in secret; and thy Father which seeth in secret shall reward thee openly.

:7   But when ye pray, use not vain repititions, as the heathen do: for they think that they shall be heard for their much speaking.

:8   Be not ye therefore like unto them: for your Father knoweth what things ye have need of, before ye ask him.

:9   After this manner therefore pray ye: Our Father which art in heaven, Hallowed be thy name.

:10   Thy kingdom come, Thy will be done in earth, as it is in heaven.

:11   Give us this day our daily bread.

:12   And forgive us our debts, as we forgive our debtors.

:13   And lead us not into temptation, but deliver us from evil: for thine is the kingdom, and the power, and the glory, for ever. Amen.

:14   For if ye forgive men their trespasses, your heavenly Father will also forgive you:

:15   But if ye forgive not men their trespasses, neither will your Father forgive your trespasses.

:16 Moreover when ye fast, be not, as the hypocrites, of a sad countenance: for they disfigure their faces, that they may appear unto men to fast. Verily I say unto you, They have their reward.

:17 But thou, when thou fastest, anoint thine head, and wash thy face;

:18 That thou appear not unto men to fast, but unto thy Father which is in secret: and thy Father, which seeth in secret, shall reward thee openly.

:19 Lay not up for yourselves treasures upon earth, where moth and rust doth corrupt, and where thieves break through and steal:

:20 But lay up for yourselves treasures in heaven, where neither moth nor rust doth corrupt, and where thieves do not break through nor steal:

:21 For where your treasure is, there will your heart be also.

:22 The light of the body is the eye: if therefore thine eye be single, thy whole body shall be full of light.

:23 But if thine eye be evil, thy whole body shall be full of darkness. If therefore the light that is in thee be darkness, how great is that darkness!

:24 No man can serve two masters: for either he will hate the one, and love the other; or else he will hold to the one, and despise the other. Ye cannot serve God and mammon.

:25 Therefore I say unto you, Take no thought for your life, what ye shall eat, or what ye shall drink; nor yet for your body, what ye shall put on. Is not the life more than meat, and the body than raiment?

:26 Behold the fowls of the air: for they sow not, neither do they reap, nor gather into barns; yet your heavenly Father feedeth them. Are ye not much better than they?

:27 Which of you by taking thought can add one cubit unto his stature?

:28 And why take ye thought for raiment? Consider the lilies of the field, how they grow; they toil not, neither do they spin:

:29 And yet I say unto you, That even Solomon in all his glory was not arrayed like one of these.

:30   Wherefore, if God so clothe the grass of the field, which to day is, and tomorrow is cast into the oven, shall he not much more clothe you, O ye of little faith?

:31   Therefore take no thought, saying, What shall we eat? or, What shall we drink? or, Wherewithal shall we be clothed?

:32   (For after all these things do the Gentiles seek:) for your heavenly Father knoweth that ye have need of all these things.

:33   But seek ye first the kingdom of God, and his righteousness; and all these things shall be added unto you.

:34   Take therefore no thought for the morrow: for the morrow shall take thought for the things of itself. Sufficient unto the day is the evil thereof.

Lev. 19:31   Regard not them that have familiar spirits, neither seek after wizards, to be defiled by them: I am the LORD your God.

20:6   And the soul that turneth after such as have familiar spirits, and after wizards, to go awhoring after them, I will even set my face against that soul, and will cut him off from among his people.

Chapter 11

THE FRUITS OF A PRAYER WARRIOR

May I Come In?

One day Jesus knocked at my door and said,
*   "May I come in?"*
And I said, "Oh, please wait Lord, just let me
*   clean up a little,*
My corners are full of sin.
Just let me sweep up the dust and scrub the floors,
*   so my house is fit for You."*
But Jesus said, "You're my beloved child, and
*   that's what I've come to help you do."*
                                    —Helen Zaguirre

Young woman, the Lord God is your answer, and He alone. There is no other answer.

The objective of this book has been an instructive one; the success of the objective being fulfilled depends upon you. The "you" concept is very important. Why? Because you, the reader, must make the final decision. You can only have peace of mind and joy of heart—if—you are willing *to be willing* to be free!

In my house of Prayer and Praise in Garden Grove, California, I must practice what I preach. Meet "my kids" and hear their testimonies (these are the fruits of a prayer warrior):

Sue:

I was born November 27, 1952 in Houston, Texas, where I grew up. By the age of fifteen I was beginning to indulge in sex sin. I became pregnant. I gave birth to a baby boy who passed away a few hours after birth. The doctors say it was a miracle that I was saved because I was hemorrhaging very badly, but through it all I would not give up. I continued living in heavy sin and trials. When I was seventeen, I was raped by my brother. As a result of war and drugs his mind was completely deranged. This was the beginning of my hating.

I grew up in the church; I always liked participating in church functions and singing in the choir. Sometimes something would hit me and I just shout and cry and praise the Lord. I had no idea that it was the Holy Spirit.

When I was nineteen, I decided to leave home and move to California. I came here with a guy I didn't love. I was just wanting to get married. It fell through. I ended up leaving the guy and moving to L.A. I lived with my cousin and her husband who was a homosexual. This was my first encounter with that type of sickness. He would get drunk and curse, and every time I went to sleep at night I could hear my cousin crying and praying to the Lord for her husband's deliverance. I stayed there until I couldn't take it anymore. I started to have a nervous breakdown. I would cry and sometimes I would almost faint under pressure. One night I was rushed to the hospital because everyone thought there was something wrong with my heart. The doctors said I needed lots of rest.

I got a job and moved in with some girls older than myself. I know it was the grace of God that kept me safe, for these girls were into witchcraft, heavy drugs, and all types of sin. I was just too dumb to know they were trying to use me and pull me down to the pit with them. I left as soon as I could.

I needed a job so I started looking for just anything. Finally I met this woman who was a well-known rock singer. She heard me sing and gave me a job singing background. I had never sung professionally in my life, but my first job was before about two thousand people. Then I started traveling all over the U.S. and Hawaii. I got more gigs and made more and more money.

Finally I met the man I thought was for me. He beat me and used me for what little money I had. He was a junkie. I didn't know it. He would give me heroin, cocaine, and anything to keep me calm, because I had become very nervous. When I'd try and stand against him, he just talked sweet to me and let me get high. I had begun to like it. I thought I couldn't live without him. I'd even wake up in the morning and find matches crossed on my head. You see, he was trying to use voodoo and take my mind. Finally, by the grace of God I broke away from him.

As time passed I went through more and more trials. Finally, I began praying, never really understanding how my prayers would be answered. One day I met a girl named Joan, a hair stylist. She prayed with me to accept the Lord. I immediately accepted Him, for I was fed up with my way of life. I was even indulging in adultery with a man because I did not want to love, I did not want to feel hurt anymore. I could not stand to be alone; I was bound up in fear. I had also become a kleptomaniac. At the time I met Joan I was working with Paul Williams, a well-known world song writer. I was making very good money. I would do concerts with all the top rock singers. I also did the vocal background arrangement for a movie. I was getting started on my way up to success and down to hell. I had everything I wanted except Jesus.

Joan introduced me to a group of Christian kids in L.A. Through those kids and Joan I met Mom Taylor. Jesus arranged it all. I came to fellowship and the next Sunday I was baptized. The Elder felt the urgency for me to move out of my apartment. They all knew how bound up in fear I was. So I moved into Mom's house. The Lord spoke to Mom and said if I used my voice for anything else but praising Him, He would take it away.

I have been here two and a half years now, and through Jesus Christ I am a completely new person inside and out. I have found my true family in Jesus. I am learning to cook and do all the things a woman of God should know. I still have a long way to go, and I will go all the way with Jesus. I am willing to lay it all on the altar and go on so that I can reach out and help that next person who has a need.

Joan:

Out of darkness into the light is where I found myself before I got a strong, tremendous unction which engulfed me, to search and to know God for the first time like never before at age nineteen. Before this spiritual desire came to know God, I was only interested in the cares of this world, a carnal level.

I began seeking after the truth, not knowing just where to obtain it. This exposed me to many false religions, but God was merciful and He protected me every step of my search for Him. I was involved in the Eastern philosophies through some close friends who were seeking to know God too. Earnestly wanting to fulfill this thirst in my spirit, I made a mistake by receiving from everybody how they thought God wanted us to fellowship and reach

Him. It "blows my mind" how now I can see just how the Lord kept me while I was in darkness trying to see the light. The experience which involved meditation through Eastern religions was a means by which I was taught through lessons would bring God's force to minister to me in the form of a close fellowship by a light appearing to me in the centered point of my forehead. I tried this because my spirit was just crying out to Jesus, and I couldn't understand it at that time. I met psychics, spiritualists and an African witch doctor through my quest for the real way to God. I did not know or understand about the right and wrong ways of the truth, or the good and evil. I thought that everything was of God, but I didn't know about the enemy of my soul, so I got into many traps.

God is good, this I knew. The witch doctor that I met was wanting to teach me about occultism, but each time he would try to talk to me about it, or just come around me, I got uncomfortable and left. One night just before he wanted to come to see me, I was so afraid and oppressed until I started calling out loud to God to help me and to protect me from evil. That night I felt very impressed to turn my TV set on, and when I did people came on praising Jesus and loving Jesus, and they were all thanking Him.

Jesus Christ came into my heart that night. The next thing I knew, I was praising and thanking Him too for saving me! Everywhere I went I told people about the love of Jesus Christ. All my old habits of drugs and sex sins are crucified on the cross, never to have another victory in my life. Amen.

Lorinda:

I was born and raised a Catholic. For as long as I can remember, I loved the Lord. Attending a Catholic school was a very fulfilling experience for me. But as I became older, the doctrine of the Catholic Church didn't make sense to me. I left the church, and I prayed a prayer, the depth of which I wouldn't comprehend until I was twenty-three. I asked God to reveal Himself to me and to keep me from false religions.

At the age of nineteen I got married in a Baptist minister's study. The guy I married was a $25-a-day drug addict. I knew this before I married him. I also got pregnant and had an abortion before I married him. I was terrified my baby would be born a drug addict. My married life was hell. I was working and supporting Teddy's drug habit. Although he never struck me physically, he struck me mentally. We would argue for three hours sometimes because I wouldn't give him money for his habit.

One Saturday I came home from my sister's house and found my apartment broken into. Our TV and component system were taken. I cried bitter, hurt tears of anguish because I felt I was trying so hard to make the best of my circumstances. Finally I became so listless and undernourished my sister was afraid for my life. I would sit for hours staring and thinking about nothing. She told me I had all the symptoms of a nervous breakdown.

She worked for a sanitarium and said she would have me committed if I didn't straighten up. This was the turning point in my life. I left Linda and moved to Philadelphia with my grandmother. I had several different jobs before I worked for Mike Douglas. I was put in contact with several people, and I began to toy with the thought of being a professional prostitute. At this point I was completely disgusted with my life, and I loved absolutely no one.

I came to L.A. for a vacation and to contact people who would give me a job traveling with a famous singer. It was foolproof in my eyes, but Jesus is supreme. Everything fell through. On December 24, 1974, I received Jesus and the Holy Spirit. I didn't ask any questions because on that day God answered my prayer of so many years.

Tammy:

I was very fortunate as a young girl because I had come from a very strong Christian family. We would attend church regularly. I had accepted Christ as my personal Saviour at the age of nine at a Billy Graham meeting.

It had taken a large amount of years for the work of Satan to start slowly turning me away from the Lord. But that's how Satan works. He will make you slip in small ways and at a slow pace where you feel you are not really falling away at all. Then he makes you feel wrong is right and right is wrong. He always makes himself appear as an angel of light.

I am now twenty-five years old, and it was not until five years ago that I realized how far away from the Lord I was. And being so deep in sin, committing adultery, taking drugs, and being married to a man I didn't love, I wound up in a mental institute because of a nervous breakdown. After that I started to lose interest in life and taking drugs again, only compounding my problems more. Through my problems with drugs I spent the last five years in and out of hospitals. I had come to a point where I almost had a reprobate mind, but even though I was so deep in sin, the Lord still had His plan for me and was waiting to intervene when I was ready to call out to Him, which happened in the month of May, 1976.

It was a Saturday night, and I had been watching a movie called "Go Ask Alice." It was about a girl who was hooked on drugs. Through watching that movie it seemed the Lord was trying to show me something. I then broke down in such a way and cried as never before. I fell on my knees and asked the Lord if He could find a way to bring me to a place where I could have Christian fellowship with people my own age. It would help me get away from the drug scene around me. Within that week my brother called asking if I would be interested in seeing about living at

Mom Taylor's. He told me it was a Christian organization. It wasn't until Friday of that week when I was on my knees asking the Lord into my heart, with Mom Taylor, my brother Bob and his wife, Beverly, at my side, that I realized the Lord had answered my prayer. I believe that He will answer strong and mightier prayers in the future. I praise Him for delivering me, not only from drugs, but from a dying mind as well. PRAISE GOD!

Larry:

In July 1, 1974, my world was falling in on me. I was so far in debt it seemed I would never get out. My marriage of four years was breaking up. My wife had filed for divorce, and that was the end of the world for me.

Having been brought up in the church, I knew there was a God and I knew He was the only one I could turn to. I cried for days and nights for help.

After weeks of crying out, the Lord led a servant of His to meet me. Just days before she had moved into an apartment near mine. After many meetings with her, I realized the Lord had answered my prayers. This sister ministered to me out of the Bible. On July 15, I gave my life to Jesus and started going to Melodyland Christian Center.

I had given up cigarettes and drinking, but there seemed to be something lacking. So on August 18, I had my first real water baptism. Though I had been "baptized" when I was a year old, it was only a sprinkle. I started going to church every Sunday and watched a Christian television in the evenings. I felt I wanted to be doing something for the Lord, so I started going to the TV station. They had just started and were asking for volunteers. While I was there, I met another faithful servant of God, Mom Taylor. One day she asked for volunteers to help clean the TV station, so I volunteered. Then I discovered that she had fellowship nights on Fridays. After attending several fellowships it wasn't long before I saw Mom Taylor was truly a woman of God.

I witnessed the love and the true teaching of the Word of God and knew that God's presence was at her house. I knew in my heart that I wanted to be a man of God, and that if I could get my heart right with God I might someday be back with my wife. I asked Mom if I could move in her house, and she said yes. I thank God that Mom said yes, because she knew the evil that was in me and knew that it was going to be hard work to help me.

Since I have been at Mom's house—I came in November, 1974—Jesus has delivered me and set me free of the homosexuality I've had since I was fourteen. Jesus has delivered me from being a psychopathic liar, which I had been since an early age. I would lie to cover up a lie to cover another lie. Jesus also washed away my stealing and embezzling traits.

I was impressed by people. Anybody with a known name, position or reputation. I would want to be near such a person, or try to impress others by knowing such and such a person. I praise my Lord Jesus and thank Him for being so good, forgiving and merciful.

Sometimes I would begin thinking of my past or not be watchful and Satan would get me bound up again. But I knew I would have to sincerely be sorry, repent and go on—always keeping my Lord and His commandments foremost in my mind. Jesus is so precious and wonderful and longsuffering with me. He is still working on me about my rebellion and pride, and some other areas, but I pray He will keep on having patience with me, and will continue to perfect me until that day when we will be like Him, when we will go home to be with Him. *I praise You, Jesus, and thank You!*

Carol:

At the age of fourteen I was pretty rebellious and thought I knew more than my parents. I just wanted to do my own thing. I started messing around with boys and having sex. Before I was eleven years old I was so curious about sex that I had lesbian sex relations with my girl friend across the street. Shortly after that I got more involved with just about any guy—having sex, drinking alcohol and going to wild parties. I didn't really care about the man, I was just out to satisfy myself. Consequently, I would seduce and entice them until they fell in love with me and then I would drop them.

Just before I graduated from high school I got pregnant. I could not tell my parents and did not want to go through the shame and trouble of having the baby, so I secretly had an abortion. Six months later I got pregnant; again I had an abortion. I tried to protect myself from having a hurt or painful experience by hardening my heart. I would not let myself have love, compassion, or even shed a tear over the abortions.

Marijuana was my next step along with more sex, smoking heavier, drinking, and taking the pill so I wouldn't have to worry any more.

I moved out of home when I was eighteen years old, my parents not suspecting a thing, still thinking I was their sweet, innocent daughter. They did not stand firm in the truth and correct me—that didn't help me at all. I walked all over them, using them in any way to help myself. I used any and everyone I could craftily and deceitfully work to my own benefit.

My sins intensified for about three years until someone told me about Jesus and invited me to their church. It was different from my old church, which I had never paid attention to anyway. Everybody was participating in song, and they all had Bibles; they showed a great interest in the

Word of God. For the first time the Word of God ministered to my heart. I received Jesus into my heart one week later.

I went on for three months. I thought I was a Christian now, but no one had told me about living a holy life. I continued in "modified" sex but started drinking and going to bars now since I was twenty-one.

One night I went to a fellowship at Mom Taylor's house. Through her the Lord showed me how to begin a holy life. That night was the turning point of my life. I turned from my sex sins and alcohol and I came to live at her home.

Through a lot of heavy counselling, prayer, much much crying out to God and the Word of God, the Lord showed me that I still had a hardened heart and that I could not love Him, or anyone else, until my heart was circumcised. He gave me this Scripture: "If thou shalt harken unto the voice of the Lord thy God, to keep His commandments and His statutes which are written in this book of the law, and if thou turn unto the Lord thy God with all thine heart, and with all thy soul . . . the Lord thy God will circumcise thine heart, and the heart of thy seed, to love the Lord thy God with all thine heart, and with all thy soul, that thou mayest live" (Deuteronomy 30:10-16).

My God is not a liar, His Word is true. He did circumcise my heart, and I love Him with all my heart and all my soul!

Everyday He teaches me through His Word, and by doing His Word He teaches me how to love others, reach out and give of myself to others, instead of using people and wanting them to do for me.

He has given me a new life and I praise Him for it. Jesus is everything to me!

Don:

Jesus first came into my life when I was in boot camp

in the Navy. It was the first time I could ever remember hearing the Gospel preached, although I had gone to church when I was younger, I never heard that Jesus could actually come into my heart and be my personal friend. Just then I needed a friend and Jesus was he. I read the Gospel of John until I got out of camp. Then at home I went back to my old sins. Still doing my own thing, I didn't read the Word anymore. Then a group of Christians on base invited me to a Bible study. Their patience and concern for me were surprising, and they were persistent. After a while, I started to read the Word again and re-dedicated my life to Jesus. As I read the Word my commitment and love for Jesus grew, and I wanted to serve Him and live a holy life. I started fasting and praying and witnessing to everyone I could. Then I met a Christian singing group that was singing in coffee shops nearby. They invited me to go with them on my weekend liberties; I went. At this time I also started to feel that for me the military was morally wrong. I prayed and sought God on this the best I knew, and then filed my papers as a conscientious objector. I was honorably discharged within six months.

I went home to see my parents for the last time. I was going to serve God full time now and be a "Jesus People." I was riding high on a pride trip. I thought I knew it all. I had a deep-seated resentment and hatred for my parents. My whole attitude was rebellious. Thank God for His mercy and grace!

Then I met Mom Taylor. My eyes were blind to all the things that I was; I was in darkness. But Mom wasn't—I know now that she saw right through me from the start. It wasn't long before I left that singing group and came to live at Mom Taylor's house. She is a woman of God, and if I didn't know anything else, I did know that. It was the mercy of God that was in Mom that let me even come to her house. A year later I went home for Christmas.

I went home to be "spiritual." Mom's carpets were tattered and torn, and she needed new ones. I had a bank account, stocks, and bonds, and a car back at home. I figured that I could just go back and get those things and be off. But my motive was wrong. I knew that doing that would crush my parents. They had scrimped and saved to put up money for my sister and I for school. They wanted us to have the "good life." They just didn't know that that life starts and is only in Jesus.

When I got home the material things that I had, and the hating, unforgiving heart in me and my pride, and a soft and easy pad, set me up. I turned into a homosexual, a child molester. It was all secret, all darkness.

But Mom Taylor knew! After being at home for two months, delaying my going back by phone calls, Mom told me that if I didn't return immediately that she wouldn't let me come back.

When I arrived at the bus station, none of the kids knew me. I was demon-possessed. But Mom had something I didn't—love. She took me into her home, prayed for me and rebuked me, and all my brothers and sisters there labored over me night and day until I got delivered. I forgave my parents and Jesus forgave me. I learned what it means to cry out to Jesus, to call on His name, and I met my Saviour. I love Jesus, and I love Mom Taylor. I love my parents, and won't go back into sin. I know what I was. I know Jesus changed me, and though I have trials and problems, I am going with Jesus.

Thank God that He deals with us! *Thank You, Jesus, for Your mercy!* **Thank you, Mom, for not giving up!**

Betty:
At the age of nine I said, "If something doesn't change, I'll kill myself." Teachers said they never understood me or knew what I was thinking. I was full of

rebellion and hate even then, and my parents didn't know what to do with me. At age twelve I started to steal, drink and smoke. When I turned fourteen I was getting loaded and having sex. My parents broke the news to me about getting a divorce, and I rebelled against the whole world. I started doing things that would bring shame and hurt. I lost all my security, if I had any.

Rebellion had control over me, and the pit of hell was my home. I became a biker and had a Hell's Angels boy friend. We shacked up, got loaded, and got into many fights. Between age fifteen and twenty-one I was loaded 95% of the time. At age eighteen I left home with another man, a heroin addict, male prostitute, and homosexual. My eyes have seen sex perversion, heroin addicts going through cold turkey and even dying, fights, prostitution, and pimps—things which would turn anybody's stomach. I had to sell drugs to eat, and many times I have slept on the streets or in cars. I wanted to get out of it all, but I didn't know how, and I thought my life ended there.

Finally, I got out and was on the run for the fear of my life. I was a sick girl. I came home and ended up with an abortion and different kinds of infections and sickness in my body. After the abortion, I had no more feelings; I was hard in my heart. I didn't want to live any more.

I tried to go straight, but it didn't work. I was soon on drugs again and into sex. My life was messed up, and I had deep problems.

I tried to kill myself; it wouldn't work. I tried to run; it didn't work. Satan had a hold on me and I was sick in body and mind. I hid out in different cities. I thought I had the flu, but developed pneumonia, various infections and had an abortion.

I was so sick it took a year to recover. During that time I thought I would go straight and be good. I couldn't be good long. I didn't know how. Drugs were still in my blood. Sex, I couldn't do without. I got quite hysterical at times. I had no self-control. Rebellion and hate had control over me. I kept wanting love and truth, but found neither. I didn't like going to church because when I went while I was young it didn't help me.

One day I decided to end my life for good because I couldn't stand to live in torment anymore. I hated myself. Well, God didn't listen to my plans and had something else going. He had my cousin invite me to be in her wedding. I thought, *This is the first wedding I've been in. I better meet the groom before the wedding. Knowing me, if I don't like him I'll ruin the wedding.* I decided to go to church with the couple and get that out of the way. I felt awful being at the church and tried to hide, but that didn't work either.

I don't remember what the preacher said, but one thing stayed with me. I felt the love of Jesus, and He reached down and took my hand way up in the air and I couldn't get it down. I found the way out of hell and torment that day and walked into love and truth; that was Jesus. I felt like a different person, and I knew He gave me a new life to live and an eternal life.

I was so excited I came home and told my friends and parents. Then came the persecutions. Nobody believed me, probably because they didn't know Jesus either. But I knew Jesus was for real and there was a new life to live. Jesus soon gave me Christian friends and a Bible. I was getting to be real happy. I didn't have much teaching the first six months, and I was having problems and falling. I started praying for a way to get out and live with Christians and learn about Jesus.

Well, wouldn't you know it. Jesus gave me a Christian home and a mother who could teach me. That is when I really began to change inside out. It was Jesus and His work that changed me and healed my body and mind. I feel cleaner and Jesus becomes more real to me every day. I still have a long way to go but Jesus says, "Believe on Me and keep My Word and you shall be saved and those who overcome to the end shall be saved. I will never leave you nor forsake you."

Yes, Jesus is the only way out of sin and hell. Jesus is the truth that I searched for all my life. He is the One who gives you a happy, peaceful life which is full of His love and for all eternity. That hate in me is turning to love, and I have a desire to live for Jesus.

George:

I was brought up in a Christian home. We attended church every week and heard the Word of God. I had a personal experience with the Lord when I was very young and knew Jesus was real.

As I grew up and entered junior high school I began to have problems with our family. My sister had gotten on drugs and had started running away from home. I saw what drugs did to my sister so I had no desire to get on drugs. But I began to get things in my heart. I would try to cover them up so no one would know.

I started having hatred and rebellion in my heart. In high school things got worse. I didn't care about life. I had no goal. I was living a double life, going to church on Sundays but not living it during the week. I wanted my family to think I was all right, but I acted differently with my friends. I finally was kicked out of high school my senior year. I was rebellious and mean, and I had a part in me that wanted to take my life. I got a gun and bullets and more than once intended to take my life.

After high school I got a job in Garden Grove at a rubber factory. I met a girl there who lived at a Christian house in Garden Grove. She introduced me to everyone and also the Elder of the house.

On October 31, 1973, Jesus really came into my heart. I heard about Him all my life, but He again became real in my heart. He delivered me from depression, confusion and hate. Jesus took my life of sin and confusion and healed my mind.

Everyone should know that going to church isn't enough. Just knowing about Jesus isn't enough. You have to have Him living in your heart! You must be born again. You must live a holy life and the Word of God.

*　*　*　*　*

Remember, young women, wise men still seek Jesus. I pray others will find Him in you as He is seen in the lives of my kids.

May the Lord always be with you!

—Mom (Julia) Taylor

DATE DUE